PAT BROWN, MBA

Financial Literacy For Architects

"From Blueprint to Bottom Line: Mastering Money at Every Stage of an Architect's Career"

ABRAM 47 BROWN

First published by AbramBrown47 2025

First edition

ISBN: 978-1-967737-38-3

This book was professionally typeset on Reedsy.
Find out more at reedsy.com

Contents

Preface

Throughout my life, I had the privilege of watching professionalism embodied every single day through my father, Tim Brown. For over 30 years, my dad practiced architecture with a level of discipline, pride, and commitment that left a lasting impression on me — not just about the work itself, but about how a professional carries themselves, no matter the project or the pressure.

Architecture, as I came to understand it through him, is not merely about drafting blueprints or erecting buildings. It is about solving real-world problems. It's about taking a vision and translating it into structures that serve people's lives — homes, schools, hospitals, libraries, places that become woven into the fabric of a community. Architects don't just shape skylines; they shape how people live, work, and interact.

And yet, despite the enormous impact architects have on the world around them, I also saw firsthand that many architects, including my father's peers, faced challenges that existed far beyond their drafting tables and job sites: financial challenges. The financial side of an architect's life — managing inconsistent income, paying off the cost of an extended education, saving for retirement, navigating the risks of owning a practice, balancing the desire to create with the necessity to earn — these were topics not often discussed, much less formally taught.

Architects spend years honing their skills. They master the balance of form and function, art and science. They manage clients, budgets, teams, and contractors. They meticulously plan and prepare for everything that can go wrong in a project. But when it comes to their own financial lives, they are often left without a map, without a solid set of plans.

That is why this book exists.

Financial Literacy for Architects is not about making architects into financial experts. It's about helping architects apply the same mindset that makes them successful in their work to their personal and professional finances. It's about showing how the principles that guide good design — thoughtful planning, structural integrity, long-term vision, attention to detail — are the very same principles that build strong financial foundations.

The truth is, no one cares more about your financial future than you do. And just like no two buildings are exactly alike, no two architects will walk the same financial path. Whether you are a recent graduate starting out in a small firm, a mid-career architect managing client relationships and firm leadership roles, a sole practitioner building your brand, or a senior architect preparing for retirement and legacy planning, you deserve a guide that respects the nuance of your journey.

Inspired by the professionalism and example of my father, this book was written to serve as your blueprint. It is a guide designed to meet you wherever you are — to give you tools, strategies, and a framework to build a financial life that supports your career, your family, and your future.

My hope is that, just as you design structures meant to endure, you will use this book to design a financial future that is equally strong, resilient, and lasting.

Financial literacy isn't just about numbers. It's about freedom, stability, and the ability to live life on your terms. It's about ensuring that the career you are building with so much care and creativity is matched by a financial foundation just as intentional.

You've spent your career designing spaces for others.

Now it's time to design something for yourself.

Let's get to work.

— Pat Brown, MBA

Why Architects Need Financial Literacy

Architects are trained to solve some of the world's most complex problems—but too often, their own financial life remains a mystery.

You can master design thinking, create environments that elevate human experience, and manage the intricacies of budgets, materials, zoning laws, and client expectations. Yet when it comes to managing money—budgeting, investing, retirement planning, navigating taxes—many architects find themselves operating without a solid blueprint.

This isn't a knock on architects.

It's a reflection of a broader truth: most highly educated professionals were never taught how money really works.

Financial literacy isn't built into architecture school curriculums. There's no "Money 101" course at most universities, no required financial planning seminars in graduate studies, and very little real-world training on how to navigate the wealth-building process once you enter the workforce.

As a result, many architects:

- Earn respectable incomes but still live project-to-project
- Delay investing out of fear of making a mistake
- Overthink every money decision and experience "financial paralysis"
- Avoid addressing taxes, insurance, or estate planning until it's too late
- Distrust working with financial advisors, assuming no one else will understand the nuances of the architecture profession

Here's the irony: architects are perfectly equipped to excel financially.

You already understand systems, trade-offs, optimization, iteration, and long-term thinking. You know how to envision the end product and reverse-engineer the steps needed to achieve it. These are the exact principles that apply to managing money.

- Budgeting is a resource allocation problem.
- Investing is a long-term design challenge with risk and reward curves.
- Retirement planning is a systems architecture project, balancing inputs, outputs, timelines, and constraints.
- Taxes are a series of if/then logic decisions with varying outcomes.
- Insurance is about probability, impact analysis, and risk mitigation.

When you view your financial life like a master plan—something you can design, test, and refine—it becomes far more manageable. You don't need to be an expert. You just need to approach it with the same intentionality and structure you bring to every project.

What's at Stake

Without financial literacy, even brilliant architects can end up:

- Trapped in firms or partnerships they no longer love because of financial obligations
- Paying unnecessary interest, fees, or penalties due to poor financial planning
- Missing out on early investment opportunities that could have compounded for decades
- Lacking the confidence to negotiate better salaries, project fees, or equity partnerships
- Approaching retirement unprepared—despite decades of hard work and creative achievement

And that's not just bad for individuals—it's bad for families, communities, and the broader profession that depends on financially stable, independent practitioners who can take risks, innovate, and push the field forward.

What's Possible

With financial literacy, architects can:

- Build wealth systematically and sustainably
- Align their income and career choices with their deepest values and life goals
- Gain the freedom to take creative risks, start firms, or retire on their own terms
- Protect their families and plan meaningful legacies
- Model smart financial behavior for the next generation of architects

Architects don't need more financial hype or get-rich-quick schemes. You need clear, honest, structured, design-minded financial guidance.

This book exists to give you exactly that.

Because when architects master their money, they don't just build wealth—they build freedom, resilience, and a legacy of intentional, thoughtful living.

It's time to apply the discipline, creativity, and precision you use in your work to your financial life. Not tomorrow. Not someday. Today.

A Word from the Author

I didn't start my career as an architect. But I've spent more than two decades working alongside architects—as a financial advisor, educator, and advocate for financial literacy. And over the years, I've noticed a frustrating pattern:

Architects are some of the most creative, disciplined, and insightful professionals I've ever met—yet they're often underprepared when it comes to money.

That disconnect stuck with me.

It wasn't because architects were careless or indifferent. It was because the financial world often speaks a language that doesn't match how architects think. It's filled with vague advice, emotional pitches, and cookie-cutter rules of thumb. There's too much noise, and not enough structure.

Meanwhile, architects are looking for logic. For systems. For design thinking. For blueprints that actually work.

That's why I made it my mission to bridge that gap.

I Believe This:

Architects deserve financial education that matches their mindset.

Not fluff. Not fear. Just smart frameworks, clear math, and practical tools.

You shouldn't have to figure it all out on your own.

You weren't taught this in school—and most financial "advice" out there either talks down to you or talks around you.

The better architects do with money, the more impact they can have.

On their families. On their communities. On the world. I've seen too many creative professionals trapped by financial stress—and too many others, once financially free, use their talents to create something bigger than themselves.

That's why this book exists.

This is more than just a profession for me. It's a calling. I believe financial literacy is the foundation for freedom, purpose, and legacy. I believe it's a right—not a luxury. And I believe architects are uniquely positioned to thrive once they're given the right tools.

If this book helps even one architect feel more confident, more empowered, and more in control of their financial future, it's worth every page.

I'm honored to walk this journey with you.

Let's build wealth—intentionally, thoughtfully, and for the long run.

— Pat Brown, MBA

Financial Literacy Advocate

Architects Don't Wing It—And Neither Should Your Financial Life

Architects don't wing it. You're trained to think critically, evaluate variables, and design systems that not only look beautiful but function under pressure. The same mindset that makes you great at architecture can be your greatest asset in building wealth—if you apply it intentionally.

This book is not about hype or hope. It's about systems, strategy, and sustainability.

It's about treating your financial life the same way you would approach a complex design challenge:

1. Start with a Clear Objective

In architecture, you begin with the end in mind. You define the client's vision, the building's purpose, the site's constraints.

Your financial life is no different.

Are you trying to become debt-free? Retire early? Build generational wealth? Open your own firm?

Start by defining your financial "specs." What does success look like for you? What are the functional and aesthetic goals of your financial design?

This will shape how you move through this book—and how you implement what you learn.

2. Respect the System Interactions

In architecture, no component exists in isolation. Every element—structure, HVAC, lighting, materials—must work in harmony.

Your finances are the same. Budgeting, debt, investing, insurance, taxes, and income—they're all interconnected.

Change one, and you may affect the others.

This book is designed with that systems thinking in mind. You'll see how each financial decision has second- and third-order consequences—just like in your designs.

3. Don't Wait for Perfect—Iterate

Architects are trained to pursue excellence. You want clean lines, functional spaces, and elegant solutions.

But money doesn't work like a final render. You'll never have all the variables fully known at once.

Instead, take a schematic design approach:

Start with a simple budget.

Begin investing even if you're not 100% sure.

Review, revise, improve over time.

Iterate like you would with a design proposal: progress over perfection.

4. Automate What Can Be Automated

Architects love efficiency—whether it's in construction processes, material selections, or project management.

Your money should be efficient, too.

Automate:

- Savings contributions
- Investment allocations
- Bill payments

- Debt repayments

Set up systems once and let them run with minimal day-to-day oversight, just like a well-specified building system.

5. Use Data and Logic—But Trust Your Values

Yes, data matters. Yes, logic matters. But your money should reflect your values, not just your spreadsheets.

Do you value creative freedom?

Do you care about designing a life that leaves time for family, community, and passion projects?

Do you envision a legacy, not just a balance sheet?

The numbers are your tools. Your *why* is your blueprint.

6. Monitor and Maintain Like a Professional

You wouldn't design a building without a plan for regular maintenance.

Financial planning is the same.

Revisit your numbers monthly. Rebalance your investments annually. Review your financial "load-bearing walls" often.

Routine maintenance may not be glamorous—but it keeps small cracks from becoming structural failures later.

7. Know When to Call in Experts

You don't handle every part of a project alone. You collaborate with engineers, contractors, landscape architects, and consultants.

Your financial life deserves the same level of professional support.

Knowing when to work with a:

- Financial advisor
- CPA

- Estate planning attorney
- Insurance professional

...is part of being a smart architect. It's not a sign of weakness—it's a sign of strategic leadership.

In Short:

Think in systems.

Start with clear specifications.

Iterate and automate.

Balance logic with values.

Maintain your plan.

Use experts when needed.

Approach your financial life like the most important, meaningful project you'll ever design—because it is.

This time, you are the client, the designer, and the builder.

So let's create a life that works—for now, and for decades to come.

How to Use This Book

This is not a book you have to read cover to cover in one sitting—nor is it meant to overwhelm you with theory without action. Think of it like a set of construction documents for your financial life: clear, detailed, and structured to help you build something lasting.

Whether you're just starting your career, running a firm, or planning for retirement, this book is designed to meet you where you are and grow with you.

Here's how to get the most out of it:

1. Think of It as a Reference Manual, Not a Novel

You wouldn't flip through a building code once and expect to have it all memorized. Likewise, this book is here for you to consult when you're facing a specific challenge or decision—whether it's negotiating a salary, managing cash flow in your firm, setting up retirement accounts, or succession planning.

Start with the sections most relevant to your stage of life or career, and circle back as your situation evolves.

2. Move at Your Own Pace

Financial literacy is a journey, not a sprint.

Each chapter builds toward a stronger financial foundation, but there's no "deadline" to have it all mastered. Focus on what's most pressing for you right now—whether that's budgeting basics or estate planning—and layer in complexity as you grow more comfortable.

3. Use It to Build Your Personal Blueprint

Throughout this book, you'll find frameworks, checklists, and action steps designed to help you create your own financial blueprint. Treat it the same way you would a design schematic: adjust for your personal goals, lifestyle, and risk tolerance.

You're not following someone else's plan. You're designing your own.

4. Focus on Systems, Not Just Goals

We all have goals: retire by 60, save for a house, build a firm.

But goals without systems are just wishes. This book emphasizes systems thinking—the same mindset you use when designing a building or a city block. We'll help you create financial systems that work automatically and adjust dynamically, just like good architecture.

5. Take Notes, Sketch Ideas, Revise Often

This isn't just about reading—it's about doing. Highlight key ideas. Jot down questions. Sketch out your first draft of a financial plan.

Like a design charette, your first pass is rarely your last. Expect to revisit, refine, and revise your financial plans as life evolves.

6. Treat Financial Literacy as Professional Development

Your ability to manage your personal and business finances is just as critical as your ability to deliver high-quality designs.

Investing time in financial literacy pays dividends—giving you more freedom, more stability, and ultimately, more creative control over your life and work.

Make it part of your ongoing professional development, just like continuing education for licensure.

7. Don't Go It Alone

Even the best architects rely on structural engineers, contractors, and consultants.

Similarly, consider this book a starting point—and know when to bring in financial advisors, accountants, estate planners, or other professionals to help you execute your vision.

There's no award for figuring everything out solo. Smart architects know the value of collaboration.

Final Word on How to Use This Book

You are the architect of your financial future.

This book is your first set of plans—a working draft to guide your design process.

Review it often. Revise as needed. Make it your own.

Because just like architecture, financial freedom doesn't happen by accident.

It's intentional.

It's designed.

It's built—brick by brick, decision by decision, plan by plan.

Part I: Foundations — Preparing in Architecture School

Architecture school demands creativity, discipline, and countless hours mastering your craft. But as you work to build your portfolio and prepare for licensure, there's another blueprint you should be drafting — your financial foundation.

In *Part I: Foundations — Preparing in Architecture School,* we dive into the essential financial skills every architecture student needs before stepping into the professional world. This section equips you with strategies to manage the high cost of education — including tuition, studio supplies, and software — while avoiding the debt traps that can burden early careers.

You'll learn how to think about student loans with a strategist's mindset, craft a realistic budget that respects both your limited income and the unique demands of architecture school, and start building credit responsibly — critical steps toward financial independence.

This part also tackles the hidden costs of pursuing licensure, including the Architect Registration Examination (ARE) fees, study materials, and the time commitment often overlooked by students focused solely on design work. We cover the pros and cons of internships, part-time work, and freelance opportunities during school — not just for the experience, but for the financial boost they can provide if handled wisely.

More importantly, this section introduces the concept of setting short-term, mid-term, and long-term financial goals even before graduation. By viewing your financial life as a design project — one that needs thoughtful planning, a phased approach, and a solid foundation — you can avoid common pitfalls and start your career with greater stability and confidence.

Part I ensures that as you prepare to design buildings, you're also preparing to design a financial life that is just as durable, intentional, and visionary as the structures you'll bring into the world.

Chapter 1: Understanding the True Cost of an Architecture Degree

The High Price of Design: A Financial Reality Check

Architecture is a calling that demands passion, creativity, and a relentless commitment to excellence. Yet, beneath the prestige of the profession lies a sobering financial truth: the cost of becoming an architect is steep, and it's often underestimated. Before the first brick is laid in a career, the foundation must be paid for — in tuition, fees, and a host of hidden expenses that few outside the field truly grasp.

To design a strong financial future, you must first understand the full investment you're making in your education. Let's break it down.

Tuition: The Starting Block

Architecture programs are notorious for being among the most expensive degrees in higher education. Public in-state universities might charge $10,000–20,000 per year for tuition, while private institutions can easily exceed $40,000–50,000 annually.

Add on the fact that most Bachelor of Architecture (B.Arch) programs span five years instead of the traditional four, and the tuition tally quickly multiplies. For those pursuing a Master of Architecture (M.Arch), especially if they come from a non-architecture undergraduate background, the additional years of study add even more cost.

Key Considerations:

- **Five-Year Commitment**: Unlike many undergraduate programs, the B.Arch degree typically demands five full years, meaning five years of tuition, fees, and living expenses.
- **Graduate School Costs**: If you opt for a separate master's program, prepare for two to three more years of high tuition rates.
- **Inflation**: Tuition tends to rise annually. Locking in a tuition guarantee plan can sometimes mitigate this risk.

Fees: The Hidden Costs Behind the Scenes

Beyond tuition, there are mandatory university fees — often for facilities, technology, labs, and student services. While these might seem small compared to tuition, they add up:

- **Technology Fees**: Architecture students rely heavily on technology. Many universities have separate fees for computer labs, printing, and software access.
- **Studio Fees**: Since architecture involves hands-on model making, material lab access, and specific studio space usage, additional fees are standard.
- **Travel and Field Trips**: Site visits and study-abroad programs, often essential to a robust architectural education, typically come at your own expense.

Hidden Costs: What's Not on the Invoice

Studio Supplies

Architecture students spend hundreds, sometimes thousands, annually on materials.

- Model-making supplies
- Sketchbooks, drafting paper
- Professional-grade pens, pencils, and markers
- Foam boards, basswood, adhesives
- Specialty tools: X-Acto knives, cutting mats, rulers

Software

Professional software licenses are a must-have:

- AutoCAD
- Revit
- Rhino
- SketchUp
- Adobe Creative Suite

Educational discounts help, but subscriptions and one-time purchases add up. Some schools provide free access; others don't.

Technology

Your standard laptop won't cut it. Expect to purchase a high-performance computer capable of handling 3D modeling and rendering — often $2,000–4,000.

Printing and Plotting

Architectural plans and presentations often require large-scale prints.

- Plotting costs can range from $10 to $100+ per project, depending on the number of boards.

Travel

If your program includes field trips, study abroad, or studio trips, you'll likely cover:

- Airfare
- Hotels
- Meals
- Transportation

These trips, while enriching, can quickly add several thousand dollars to your education tab.

Licensure Preparation

Even before you graduate, preparing for the Architect Registration Examination (ARE) comes with costs:

- Study materials
- Practice exams
- Prep courses

Licensure is mandatory to practice as an architect in most places, and early preparation is wise — but not cheap.

Budgeting During School: Surviving the Financial Gauntlet

Architecture school is intense, both academically and financially. Here's how to create a budget that respects both.

Fixed Expenses

- Tuition and fees
- Rent and utilities
- Food and groceries
- Transportation (car payments, gas, insurance, or public transit)

Variable Expenses

- Studio supplies (can fluctuate dramatically by semester)
- Software renewals
- Travel for projects or study abroad
- Health insurance

Smart Tips for Architecture Students

- **Secondhand Supplies**: Buy used textbooks and materials.
- **Digital First**: Where possible, invest in digital tools to reduce printing costs.
- **Shared Resources**: Pool resources with classmates for bulk materials.
- **Financial Aid Office**: Regularly check for updated scholarships and emergency grants.
- **Work-Study Jobs**: If your program allows, find a campus job, ideally in a related field like the design lab or art shop.

Budgeting while in school is less about cutting joy and more about managing unavoidable costs wisely.

Scholarships, Grants, and Financial Aid Strategies

The cost of an architecture degree can be daunting, but there are ways to reduce the financial load.

Merit-Based Scholarships

Most schools offer scholarships based on academic performance, portfolio reviews, and entrance interviews.

- **Portfolio Scholarships**: Strong portfolios can attract significant awards.
- **Merit Awards**: High GPA and standardized test scores can lead to merit aid.

Need-Based Aid

Completing the FAFSA is critical. Even private schools use it to determine need-based aid.

- **Grants**: Federal Pell Grants, state grants, and university-specific grants don't require repayment.
- **Work-Study Programs**: Provide part-time employment opportunities.

External Scholarships

Several organizations offer scholarships specifically for architecture students:

- American Institute of Architects (AIA)
- Association of Collegiate Schools of Architecture (ACSA)
- National Organization of Minority Architects (NOMA)

- Local AIA chapters and community foundations

Assistantships

Graduate students may qualify for teaching or research assistantships, often covering tuition and providing stipends.

Employer Sponsorship

Some firms offer scholarships or tuition assistance to students who intern with them.

Action Steps: Architecting Your Financial Plan

1. **Research Total Costs**: Don't just look at tuition — add up studio supplies, software, travel, and living expenses.
2. **Build a Budget**: Create a realistic, flexible budget that includes academic year and summer months.
3. **Maximize Scholarships**: Apply for as many internal and external scholarships as possible.
4. **Minimize Debt**: Borrow only what is necessary. Choose federal loans first for better repayment options.
5. **Invest in the Right Tools**: Buy a high-performance computer and software strategically.
6. **Plan for Licensure**: Start saving early for ARE costs.
7. **Track Expenses**: Use a spreadsheet or app to monitor spending.

Real-World Scenario

Imagine this:

You're accepted into a top-tier architecture program. Tuition is $30,000 a year. Studio supplies add $2,000 annually. Software subscriptions are $500 a year. You have one major studio trip costing $2,500 in your third year.

Over five years:

- Tuition: $150,000
- Studio Supplies: $10,000
- Software: $2,500
- Travel: $2,500

Total Estimated Cost: $165,000 (before rent, food, transportation, and other living expenses).

Without scholarships or aid, that's a heavy debt load. Understanding this early allows you to seek financial aid aggressively and make informed decisions.

Pros and Cons of Financing Options

Student Loans

Pros:

- Immediate access to funds.
- Federal loans offer income-driven repayment.

Cons:

- Long-term debt burden.
- Interest accrues, increasing total repayment.

Scholarships and Grants

Pros:

- Free money that doesn't require repayment.

Cons:

- Highly competitive.
- May require maintenance of GPA or other commitments.

Part-Time Work

Pros:

- Helps cover living expenses.

Cons:

- May interfere with demanding studio schedules.

Final Thoughts

Pursuing a degree in architecture is one of the most rewarding journeys you can embark on, but it requires careful financial planning. Understand the true cost, budget smartly, pursue all available aid, and borrow cautiously.

You are not just investing in a degree — you are investing in your future as a designer, a thinker, and a leader.

You are more capable than you think — and you're building a future you can be proud of.

Financial planning isn't about being perfect — it's about laying a solid foundation and refining it over time.

The smartest architects don't just design beautiful buildings — they design sustainable lives.

Keep reviewing and updating your financial blueprint as your education progresses.

Let's build something lasting.

Chapter 2: Managing Student Debt Before Graduation

Facing Reality: The Importance of Early Debt Management

Architecture is a long journey — and not just academically. Financially, the path is demanding from day one. With the cost of an architecture degree often exceeding six figures, managing student debt must be treated with the same thoughtfulness and precision you bring to your design work.

Waiting until after graduation to deal with your loans is like building a structure and ignoring the foundation. Planning starts now.

Understanding the Loan Landscape

Before you can manage student debt, you need to know what you're dealing with.

Federal Loans vs. Private Loans

Federal Loans

Federal student loans are issued by the government and come with several benefits:

- **Fixed Interest Rates**: These loans have interest rates set by Congress, which remain constant over the life of the loan.
- **Flexible Repayment Options**: Income-driven repayment plans, deferment, forbearance, and loan forgiveness programs are only available with federal loans.
- **Subsidized vs. Unsubsidized**:
- **Subsidized** loans do not accrue interest while you're enrolled at least half-time.
- **Unsubsidized** loans accrue interest immediately.

Private Loans

Private loans are offered by banks, credit unions, and other financial institutions.

- **Variable or Fixed Rates**: Interest rates can fluctuate.
- **Less Flexibility**: Repayment terms are stricter; deferment or forbearance may not be an option.
- **Credit-Based**: Approval and interest rates are often based on your credit score and history.

Key Differences

Federal loans tend to be safer for students because they provide more breathing room post-graduation. Private loans may offer lower interest rates initially, but they lack the safety net of government-backed protections.

Action Step

Before taking out a private loan, exhaust all federal loan options.

How Interest Accrues in School: The Silent Cost

Interest is the cost of borrowing money, and it starts accumulating before most students even realize it.

Interest on Subsidized Loans

- Interest does not accrue while you're enrolled at least half-time.
- The government pays the interest during in-school deferment and grace periods.

Interest on Unsubsidized Loans

- Interest begins accruing as soon as the loan is disbursed.
- If you do not pay the interest while in school, it capitalizes — meaning it's added to the principal, and future interest is calculated on the new, higher balance.

Private Loan Interest

- Most private loans begin accruing interest immediately.
- Some private lenders allow interest-only payments while in school.

The Cost of Waiting

Ignoring interest while you're in school can cost you thousands. Let's break it down.

Example:

- Loan amount: $30,000
- Interest rate: 5%
- School years: 5

Simple math (not even compounding) shows:

$30,000 x 0.05 = $1,500 interest per year

$1,500 x 5 = $7,500 total interest accrued during school.

Ignoring that interest means graduating with $37,500 in debt instead of $30,000.

Action Step

If possible, make interest-only payments while in school. Even small payments can prevent interest from ballooning.

Repayment Strategies to Plan for Now

The best time to start thinking about repayment isn't after you graduate — it's right now.

Know What You Owe

Start by listing all your loans:

- Lender name
- Loan amount
- Interest rate
- Subsidized or unsubsidized
- Payment status (in deferment, forbearance, etc.)

Use a simple spreadsheet or a financial app designed for students.

Action Step

Request your complete loan information from the National Student Loan Data System (NSLDS) for federal loans and from your private lenders.

Understand Your Grace Period

Most federal student loans offer a six-month grace period after graduation before repayment begins.

- **Subsidized Loans**: No interest accrues during the grace period.
- **Unsubsidized Loans**: Interest continues accruing.

Private loans' grace periods vary widely, and some may not have any at all.

Action Step

Mark the end of your grace period on your calendar. Plan to make your first payment before it's due to establish good habits.

Choose the Right Repayment Plan

Federal Loan Repayment Options

- **Standard Repayment Plan**: Fixed payments over 10 years.
- **Graduated Repayment Plan**: Payments start lower and increase every two years.
- **Income-Driven Repayment Plans**:
- Income-Based Repayment (IBR)
- Pay As You Earn (PAYE)
- Revised Pay As You Earn (REPAYE)
- Income-Contingent Repayment (ICR)

These plans cap payments at a percentage of your discretionary income.

Private Loan Repayment

Options vary, but most private lenders offer:

- Standard repayment
- Interest-only payments
- Full deferment (interest accrues)

Action Step

Before graduation, use loan simulators to estimate monthly payments under different plans.

To Refinance or Not: Evaluating the Options

Pros of Refinancing

- Potentially lower interest rates
- Simplified repayment (one loan instead of several)

Cons of Refinancing Federal Loans

- Loss of federal protections (income-driven repayment, forbearance, deferment)
- Not eligible for Public Service Loan Forgiveness (PSLF)

Action Step

Only refinance if you have stable income, excellent credit, and no need for federal loan benefits.

Aggressive vs. Conservative Repayment

Aggressive Strategy

- Pay more than the minimum monthly payment.
- Focus on highest-interest loans first (avalanche method).

Conservative Strategy

- Stick to minimum payments and invest extra cash elsewhere.
- Use income-driven plans if cash flow is tight.

Action Step

Decide early: Is your goal to be debt-free quickly or to balance loan payments with other financial goals like saving for retirement?

Building Your Pre-Graduation Financial Plan

It's not just about graduating — it's about graduating with a plan.

1. **Calculate Your Estimated Debt Load**: How much will you owe at graduation?
2. **Estimate Your First-Year Salary**: Research average salaries for architecture grads in your area.
3. **Draft a Preliminary Budget**: Allocate portions of your future salary to rent, food, transportation, loan payments, and savings.
4. **Create a Debt Payoff Timeline**: Map out when you want to be debt-free.

Real-World Scenario

Imagine this:

You graduate with $80,000 in federal student loans and $20,000 in private loans.

Your federal loans average 5% interest. Your private loan is 7%.

Your starting salary is $58,000.

Without a plan:

- Payments may feel crushing.

With a plan:

- Standard federal loan payment: ~$850/month.
- Private loan payment: ~$250/month.
- Total: $1,100/month.

By sticking to this and applying bonuses, raises, and side income, you can pay off loans in under 10 years.

Pros and Cons of Early Repayment

Pros

- Save thousands in interest.
- Gain financial freedom sooner.
- Less debt stress.

Cons

- May divert funds from investing.
- Opportunity cost if investments outperform loan interest.

Final Thoughts

Managing student debt before graduation is not a burden — it's an opportunity to design your financial future with intention and care.

Understanding your loans, minimizing interest accrual, and creating a realistic repayment plan are critical steps in building a stable foundation for the life and career you envision.

You are more capable than you think — and you're building a future you can be proud of.

Financial planning isn't about being perfect — it's about laying the groundwork and refining it over time.

The smartest architects don't just design beautiful buildings — they design sustainable lives.

Keep reviewing and updating your financial blueprint as your education progresses.

Let's continue building something lasting.

Chapter 3: Setting Financial Goals Before You Graduate

The Power of Early Planning: Why Goals Matter

In architecture, everything begins with a plan. Before a single line is drawn or a foundation is poured, architects envision the final structure — not just in its form but in its function, its resilience, and its impact. The same principle holds true for your financial life.

Setting financial goals before you graduate is not an exercise in wishful thinking. It's the blueprint for the financial house you'll live in for the rest of your career. Without a clear plan, it's too easy to drift into debt, lifestyle inflation, and financial stress.

Goals bring clarity. They give you a direction and a metric by which to measure progress.

Thinking About Money with a Project Management Mindset

In architecture, project management is about defining scope, time, and cost. Financial planning follows a similar pattern:

- **Scope**: What are you trying to achieve?
- **Time**: When do you want to achieve it?
- **Cost**: What resources will it take?

By applying the project management mindset to your finances, you're able to bring the same discipline to your money that you bring to your work.

The Three-Tiered Goal System: Short-Term, Mid-Term, and Long-Term Goals

Just as you wouldn't try to build a skyscraper overnight, you shouldn't try to achieve every financial goal at once. Effective financial planning breaks goals into three timeframes.

Short-Term Goals (0-3 Years)

These are your immediate priorities, typically achievable within three years.

Common Short-Term Goals:

- Building an emergency fund.
- Paying off small high-interest debts.
- Buying a reliable computer and software for work.
- Saving for a security deposit and initial rent for your first post-graduation apartment.
- Creating a basic budget.

Why They Matter

Short-term goals lay the groundwork. They create financial stability and prevent small problems from becoming major setbacks.

Action Steps:

- Open a separate savings account for your emergency fund.
- Set up auto-transfers from checking to savings.
- Track all expenses to identify and eliminate unnecessary spending.

Mid-Term Goals (3-7 Years)

Mid-term goals require more planning and discipline.

Common Mid-Term Goals:

- Paying down significant portions of student loan debt.
- Saving for a down payment on a home.
- Earning professional licensure (ARE exams and associated costs).
- Buying a car if necessary.
- Investing in continuing education or certifications.

Why They Matter

Mid-term goals are the "load-bearing walls" of your financial structure. They support your stability and growth.

Action Steps:

- Map out a repayment plan for student loans.
- Research first-time homebuyer programs.
- Budget for ARE exam fees and prep courses.
- Allocate a portion of every raise or bonus to these goals.

Long-Term Goals (7+ Years)

Long-term goals are your "architectural vision" — the bigger picture.

Common Long-Term Goals:

- Saving for retirement.
- Building a portfolio of investments.
- Starting your own firm.
- Saving for your children's education.
- Planning for financial independence.

Why They Matter

Long-term goals ensure that your financial structure will stand the test of time.

Action Steps:

- Open a retirement account (401(k), IRA).
- Learn the basics of investing.
- Create a "Firm Launch Fund" if entrepreneurship is a goal.
- Start small but consistent contributions to long-term savings.

Goal Setting with the SMART Framework

In project management, goals must be SMART:

- **Specific**: Define exactly what you want.
- **Measurable**: Know how you'll track progress.
- **Achievable**: Be realistic.
- **Relevant**: Align with your personal and professional values.
- **Time-bound**: Set deadlines.

Example:

- "Save $1,500 for a professional laptop by May 2025" is a SMART goal.
- "Get better at saving money" is not.

Action Step:

Write down three SMART goals in each timeframe.

Pros and Cons of Goal Setting

Pros

- Provides clarity and focus.
- Motivates and drives better decisions.
- Reduces stress by creating a plan.

Cons

- Goals can feel restrictive if not reviewed and adjusted.
- Life changes may require goal adjustments.

Real-World Scenario

Imagine this:

You're a final-year architecture student with $60,000 in student loans, no savings, and a desire to launch your own firm one day.

Without goals:

- You graduate, take a job, and drift financially.

With goals:

- You build a $5,000 emergency fund within two years.
- You pay off $20,000 in loans within five years.
- You save $25,000 toward starting your firm within eight years.

It's the difference between living reactively and living proactively.

Building Your Financial "Master Plan"

Step 1: Conduct a Financial Site Analysis

- What are your current assets and liabilities?
- What is your cash flow — income vs. expenses?

Step 2: Draft Preliminary Financial Goals

- List out short, mid, and long-term goals.

Step 3: Create Phased Development Plans

- Break big goals into smaller, manageable phases.
- Set quarterly milestones.

Step 4: Budget to Support Goals

- Align your spending with your goals.
- Cut costs where possible; reallocate to savings.

Step 5: Monitor and Adjust

- Review progress quarterly.
- Adjust goals based on changes in income or life circumstances.

The Project Management Mindset: Money as a Living Blueprint

Great architecture is never static; it evolves. Your financial plan should, too.

- **Schematics Phase**: Define broad financial goals.
- **Design Development**: Flesh out timelines and resources.
- **Construction Documents**: Solidify the steps and action plans.
- **Build Phase**: Execute.
- **Punch List**: Review, revise, refine.

Treat your financial life as a project worthy of professional-level planning.

Action Steps to Start Now

1. **Create Your First Financial Goal List**: Short, mid, and long-term.
2. **Open a High-Yield Savings Account**: For short-term savings.
3. **Automate Your Savings**: Set up automatic transfers.
4. **Learn About Retirement Accounts**: Start contributing early.
5. **Track Your Progress**: Use spreadsheets or apps.
6. **Revisit Goals Annually**: Adjust for life changes.

Final Thoughts

Setting financial goals before you graduate is one of the smartest moves you can make. It gives you direction, control, and confidence as you step into the professional world.

Financial goals aren't about restriction; they're about intention.

You are more capable than you think — and you're building a future you can be proud of.

Financial planning isn't about being perfect — it's about laying the groundwork and refining it over time.

The smartest architects don't just design beautiful buildings — they design sustainable lives.

Keep reviewing and updating your financial blueprint as your life evolves.

Let's continue building something lasting.

Chapter 4: The Architect's Starter Financial Toolkit

Building Your Financial Foundation

Every architect knows the importance of starting with a solid foundation. Without one, even the most brilliant design is at risk of collapse. Your financial life is no different. Before you step into the professional world, you need a basic set of tools — a starter financial toolkit — to ensure that your finances are structurally sound and built to endure.

The right bank accounts, the right credit cards, and the right budgeting tools are the foundation stones of your financial structure. Like a good set of blueprints, they will guide and support you as you build toward bigger financial goals.

Bank Accounts: Your Financial Command Center

When it comes to your money, think of your bank accounts as the site office for your financial project. It's where money comes in, is organized, and is distributed to various needs.

Checking Accounts: The Day-to-Day Workhorse

Purpose

Your checking account is the hub for daily transactions. It's where your paycheck will land and from where your bills will be paid.

What to Look For

- **No Monthly Fees**: Many banks offer fee-free student or young adult checking accounts.
- **ATM Access**: Nationwide ATM networks to avoid out-of-network fees.
- **Online and Mobile Banking**: Easy access to your funds and simple bill pay features.
- **Overdraft Protection**: Some accounts link to a savings account or offer low-cost overdraft protection.

Pro Tip

Automate as much as possible — direct deposit for your paycheck, automatic bill pay for recurring expenses.

High-Yield Savings Accounts: Grow Your Safety Net

Purpose

A high-yield savings account is where you should park your emergency fund and savings for short-term goals.

What to Look For

- **High Interest Rates**: Look for accounts offering at least 10x the national average interest rate.
- **No Monthly Fees**: Avoid any account that charges you to save.
- **Easy Transfers**: Make sure you can quickly move money between your checking and savings.

Pro Tip

Keep your emergency fund in a separate high-yield savings account to resist the temptation to "borrow" from it.

Choosing the Right Bank

Big banks, online banks, and credit unions all have different advantages.

- **Big Banks**: Convenience, widespread ATM networks.
- **Online Banks**: Higher interest rates, lower fees.
- **Credit Unions**: Lower fees, community focus, personalized service.

Action Step

Open a no-fee checking account linked to a high-yield savings account before graduation.

Credit Cards: Laying the Groundwork for Your Financial Reputation

Credit cards aren't just plastic; they're tools for building your credit score — your financial reputation.

The Role of Credit in Your Financial Blueprint

Your credit score will impact:

- Apartment rentals
- Mortgage approvals
- Car loans
- Insurance premiums
- Even job offers (some employers check credit reports)

Building a positive credit history early is one of the smartest moves you can make.

Student-Friendly Credit Cards

Look for cards designed for students or young professionals.

What to Look For

- **No Annual Fee**: There's no need to pay for a card.
- **Low or 0% Introductory APR**: Helpful if you carry a small balance (though paying in full is best).
- **Cash Back or Rewards**: 1%-2% on everyday purchases.
- **Credit Reporting**: Ensure the card reports to all three major credit bureaus.

Good Options

- Student cards from major issuers like Discover, Capital One, or Chase.
- Secured cards if you have no credit history (secured by a refundable deposit).

How to Use It

- Only charge what you can afford to pay off in full each month.
- Set up autopay for at least the minimum payment to avoid late fees.
- Keep your credit utilization below 30% of your limit.

Action Step

Apply for a student credit card, use it for a few small monthly expenses (like Netflix or gas), and pay it off in full.

Budgeting Apps and Tools: Your Project Management Software

Just like architects use software to manage complex projects, you need financial tools to manage your money.

Why You Need a Budget

A budget is not about restriction; it's about direction. It's a plan that ensures you are spending in line with your values and goals.

Top Budgeting Tools for Students and Young Architects

Mint

- Free.
- Automatically syncs to your bank accounts.
- Provides spending insights.

YNAB (You Need A Budget)

- Paid, but extremely effective.
- Focuses on "giving every dollar a job."
- Great for people who want to be very hands-on.

PocketGuard

- Simplified budgeting.
- Focuses on showing how much 'spendable' money you have after bills.

Spreadsheet Budgeting

- Google Sheets or Excel.
- Totally customizable.
- Great if you want full control and a visual map.

Pro Tip

Pick a budgeting tool that fits your personality. Some people love apps; others prefer spreadsheets.

How to Build a Basic Budget

- **Calculate Your Income**
- Include all sources — part-time jobs, scholarships, financial aid refunds.
- **List Fixed Expenses**
- Rent, utilities, transportation, insurance.
- **Estimate Variable Expenses**
- Food, entertainment, supplies.
- **Set Savings Goals**
- Emergency fund, travel, ARE exam fees.

- **Track and Adjust**
- Review your budget monthly and tweak it as needed.

Action Step

Choose one budgeting app or method and set it up before graduation.

Pros and Cons of Different Financial Tools

Checking Accounts

Pros:

- Easy access to money.
- FDIC insured.

Cons:

- Low or no interest.
- Possible fees if minimums aren't met.

High-Yield Savings

Pros:

- Higher interest than traditional savings.
- Safe and insured.

Cons:

- Limited transactions per month.

Credit Cards

Pros:

- Builds credit history.
- Rewards programs.

Cons:

- Can lead to debt if mismanaged.
- High interest rates on unpaid balances.

Budgeting Apps

Pros:

- Easy tracking.
- Real-time insights.

Cons:

- May require linking sensitive information.

Real-World Scenario

Imagine this:

You're a graduating student. You have $500 in your checking account and $50 in savings. You use a debit card for everything, but you've never had a credit card. You have no real budget.

Without a toolkit:

- You continue living paycheck to paycheck.
- You struggle to get approved for your first apartment or car loan.

With a toolkit:

- You have a checking and high-yield savings account.
- You've built a 3-month emergency fund.
- You have a 720 credit score.
- You're tracking expenses and adjusting your budget monthly.

It's the difference between financial fragility and financial resilience.

The Blueprint for Your Starter Financial Toolkit

1. **Open a No-Fee Checking Account**
2. **Open a High-Yield Savings Account**
3. **Apply for a Student or Secured Credit Card**
4. **Choose a Budgeting Tool**
5. **Set Financial Goals**
6. **Automate Savings and Bill Payments**

Final Thoughts

Your starter financial toolkit is the cornerstone of your financial architecture. Just like you wouldn't design a building without the right software and tools, you shouldn't approach your financial life without the right accounts, credit, and budgeting systems.

Build this toolkit now, and it will serve you for decades to come.

You are more capable than you think — and you're building a future you can be proud of.

Financial planning isn't about being perfect — it's about laying the groundwork and refining it over time.

The smartest architects don't just design beautiful buildings — they design sustainable lives.

Keep reviewing and updating your financial blueprint as your life evolves.

Let's continue building something lasting.

Chapter 5: Internships, Part-Time Work, and Side Hustles

Earning While Learning: The Financial Reality for Architecture Students

Balancing an architecture education with earning money is not a luxury — it's often a necessity. With the high cost of tuition, studio supplies, and living expenses, most architecture students cannot afford to ignore the financial realities pressing in around them.

Yet, the demands of architecture school are intense. Studio courses are notorious for their workload and unpredictable hours. Trying to maintain a job without sacrificing academic performance or mental health requires strategy and discipline.

The good news? With thoughtful planning, it's possible to make money while preserving your studio time and academic success.

Internships: Experience and Earnings

Internships are the first real bridge between education and practice. They offer not just experience but a paycheck — or at least they should.

Finding the Right Internship

Paid vs. Unpaid

Always prioritize paid internships. Your time and labor are valuable. While some firms still offer unpaid internships under the guise of "experience," you should be compensated.

What to Look For

- **Relevant Work**: Internships that offer design work, client exposure, or construction documentation experience.
- **Flexible Hours**: Particularly during the academic year, you need a firm that understands your primary commitment is school.
- **Learning Opportunities**: You're there to learn, not just to perform grunt work.

How to Balance an Internship with Studio

- **Set Clear Boundaries**: Communicate your studio schedule clearly to your employer.
- **Manage Your Time Like a Project Manager**: Block your calendar to protect key studio hours.
- **Prioritize Health**: Overloading yourself can lead to burnout, which hurts both work and school.

Part-Time Work: Outside the Studio Walls

If internships aren't available or don't fit your schedule, part-time work is a solid option.

Best Part-Time Jobs for Architecture Students

On-Campus Jobs

- Lab assistant in the architecture department.
- Library assistant.
- Campus design or marketing teams.

Off-Campus Jobs

- Retail or service industry jobs with flexible scheduling.
- Freelance drafting or 3D modeling for local firms.
- Tutoring design software or portfolio prep for younger students.

Remote Jobs

- Online tutoring.
- Content creation for architecture blogs or firms.
- CAD or Revit modeling as a freelancer.

Key Considerations

- Flexibility is key — look for jobs that understand academic priorities.
- Low stress outside of work hours. You can't afford to bring job stress into the studio.

Action Step

Before accepting any job, map your weekly schedule to ensure you have enough time for studio work, rest, and personal health.

Side Hustles: Freelance and Beyond

Architecture students possess marketable skills that can be turned into income.

Freelance Work for Architecture Students

Opportunities

- Drafting services for local contractors.
- 3D rendering for small firms.
- Graphic design (logos, presentations).
- Portfolio reviews for younger students.
- Social media management for design firms.

How to Navigate Freelance Work

Setting Rates

Charge based on skill level and local market rates. Research what entry-level drafters or designers earn per hour.

Contracts and Agreements

Always have a basic contract, even for small projects. It should cover:

- Scope of work.
- Deliverables.
- Timeline.
- Payment terms.

Managing Taxes

Freelance income is considered self-employment income.

- Track all income.
- Save 25-30% of your freelance earnings for taxes.
- Consider quarterly estimated tax payments if earnings are significant.

Pros and Cons of Freelance Work

Pros

- Higher earning potential per hour.
- Build a professional portfolio.
- Flexible scheduling.

Cons

- Unstable income.
- Responsibility for finding clients.
- Managing taxes and contracts.

Time Management: The Key to Success

Working while in school demands excellent time management skills.

Strategies

- **Use a Planner**: Track all deadlines (school and work).
- **Batch Tasks**: Group similar activities to maximize efficiency.
- **Protect Studio Time**: Treat it like a non-negotiable work meeting.
- **Prioritize Sleep**: You can't afford to compromise your health.

Real-World Scenario

Imagine this:

You're a third-year architecture student. You intern 10 hours a week at a local firm, tutor freshmen on weekends, and freelance a few rendering projects per semester.

Without a plan:

- You miss deadlines.
- Your health and grades suffer.

With a plan:

- You schedule work hours carefully.
- You block studio time as sacred.
- You maintain a 3.5 GPA, a professional portfolio, and a growing bank account.

It's the difference between chaos and control.

Tax Essentials for Student Freelancers

Key Concepts

- **Self-Employment Tax**: You are responsible for both the employee and employer portion.
- **Estimated Taxes**: Required if you expect to owe $1,000 or more.
- **Write-Offs**: You can deduct business-related expenses like software subscriptions, part of your internet bill, and home office space.

Action Step

Consult with a CPA experienced in working with freelancers or use tax software designed for self-employed individuals.

Legal and Financial Protection

Business Structure

As a freelancer, you are a sole proprietor by default. For more protection, consider forming an LLC.

Insurance

Professional liability insurance might seem unnecessary now but could be crucial if you expand freelance work.

Pros and Cons: Internships, Part-Time Jobs, Side Hustles

Internships

Pros:

- Real-world experience.
- Networking.

Cons:

- May have low pay.
- Limited hours available.

Part-Time Jobs

Pros:

- Stable income.
- Lower responsibility levels.

Cons:

- Less relevant experience.
- Fixed schedules.

Side Hustles

Pros:

- High flexibility.
- Build portfolio and skills.

Cons:

- Unstable income.
- Complex taxes.

Action Steps to Begin

1. **Audit Your Skills**: Identify what you can offer.
2. **Set Income Goals**: Know how much you need to earn.
3. **Create a Time Budget**: Map your week.
4. **Apply for Internships**: Focus on paid opportunities.
5. **Consider Freelance Work**: Start small.
6. **Track Income and Expenses**: Use apps like QuickBooks Self-Employed.

7. **Plan for Taxes**: Save a percentage of freelance earnings.

Final Thoughts

Balancing work and school as an architecture student is tough, but it's doable with intention and planning. Internships, part-time work, and side hustles can give you financial breathing room and jumpstart your career.

Remember, it's not about doing everything. It's about doing the right things, with the right structure, at the right time.

You are more capable than you think — and you're building a future you can be proud of.

Financial planning isn't about being perfect — it's about laying the groundwork and refining it over time.

The smartest architects don't just design beautiful buildings — they design sustainable lives.

Keep reviewing and updating your financial blueprint as your life evolves.

Let's continue building something lasting.

Chapter 6: Professional Licensing and Exam Costs

The Architect's Gateway: Why Licensure Matters

In architecture, licensure is more than a professional milestone — it is the foundation of your legal ability to call yourself an architect and practice independently. Without a license, you're limited in responsibility, authority, and career progression.

Yet, earning that license is not just about passing exams. It requires a financial commitment that many underestimate. The Architect Registration Examination (ARE) and its associated costs can quickly add up.

Understanding these costs ahead of time gives you the power to plan for them, minimize financial stress, and integrate licensure seamlessly into your broader career and financial blueprint.

The Financial Roadmap for the AREs

The ARE is a series of six divisions designed to assess your knowledge and skills in architecture.

Exam Division Fees

Each division costs $235 to $285, depending on the testing year and updates by the National Council of Architectural Registration Boards (NCARB).

At an average of $235 per division:

- 6 divisions x $235 = $1,410 total.

If you need to retake any division, that's another $235 per attempt.

NCARB Record Maintenance

To sit for the ARE, you must maintain an active NCARB Record.

- Application fee: Around $100-$200.
- Annual renewal: Around $85/year.

The NCARB Record is your official transcript of education, experience (AXP), and examination.

State Licensure Fees

Once you pass the ARE, you still have to apply for licensure at the state level.

- Application fees range from $100 to $300.
- License issuance fees can add another $100.

Annual or biennial renewal fees typically range from $100 to $250.

Example: Typical Costs

- ARE Exams: ~$1,410
- NCARB Record Setup: $100
- NCARB Annual Renewal (1 year): $85
- State Licensure Application: $200
- Initial License Fee: $100

Total Estimated Cost: ~$1,895

This does not include study materials, prep courses, travel expenses, or retake fees.

Budgeting for Test Prep, Materials, and Fees

Passing the ARE is not just about sitting for the exam. Preparation is key, and that preparation carries its own costs.

Study Materials

ARE 5.0 Prep Materials

- Books: $50–$100 per division.
- Online subscriptions (Black Spectacles, Pluralsight): $50–80/month.
- Practice Exams: $100–200.

Prep Courses

If self-study isn't enough, live or online courses are available.

- Bootcamps or seminars: $300–500 per division.
- Full prep packages: $2,000–4,000.

Additional Expenses

- **Software**: Access to practice software for case studies and simulations.
- **Travel**: If testing centers aren't close to your residence.
- **Time**: Lost wages if you reduce work hours to study.

Total Prep Costs Estimate

- Study materials: $600–1,200
- Practice exams: $300–600
- Prep courses: $2,000–4,000 (optional)

Budgeting a total of **$3,000–5,000** for prep alone is not uncommon.

Hidden Costs: Retakes and Time

Failing an exam is costly:

- Retake Fee: $235 per division.
- Additional study material or course costs.
- Delay in professional advancement and salary increases.

Some candidates take 18-24 months to pass all sections, depending on workload and life balance.

Planning Your Financial Path to Licensure

Step 1: Create a Licensure Budget

1. List all fixed costs: Exam fees, NCARB fees, state fees.
2. Estimate variable costs: Study materials, courses, travel.
3. Add a buffer for retakes and unexpected expenses.

Sample Budget

- ARE Exams: $1,410
- NCARB Setup + Renewal: $185
- State Licensure: $300
- Study Materials + Courses: $3,000
- Buffer: $500

Total: ~$5,395

Step 2: Set a Timeline

Most candidates aim to complete all divisions within 12-18 months. Set a realistic schedule based on:

- Work commitments.
- Family responsibilities.
- Financial readiness.

Step 3: Save Strategically

Treat licensure as a project.

- Open a dedicated savings account.
- Set automatic monthly savings goals.
- Use bonuses, tax refunds, or freelance income to accelerate savings.

Step 4: Employer Assistance

Some firms reimburse exam costs or offer bonuses for licensure.

- Ask about reimbursement policies.
- Some firms cover study material costs.

Step 5: Minimize Costs Where Possible

- Buy used or shared study materials.
- Form a study group to split costs.
- Use free resources like NCARB's practice exams.

Real-World Scenario

Imagine this:

You're a junior architect earning $58,000 per year. You budget $300 per month toward licensure costs.

In 18 months:

- $300 x 18 = $5,400

You've covered all fees, materials, and buffer costs without debt.

Without a plan:

- You're scrambling for credit cards or loans.
- Stress compromises your ability to study effectively.

With a plan:

- You pass all divisions in 18 months.
- You're licensed and negotiating a $10,000 salary increase.

Pros and Cons of the Financial Commitment

Pros

- Long-term earning potential increases.
- Professional credibility.
- Ability to stamp drawings and take on bigger responsibilities.

Cons

- High upfront costs.
- Time-consuming study periods.
- Potential for financial strain if unprepared.

Action Steps to Start

1. **Research your state's licensure requirements.**
2. **Calculate the full cost of exams and prep.**
3. **Open a savings account dedicated to licensure.**
4. **Create a study schedule with financial milestones.**
5. **Explore employer reimbursement options.**
6. **Consider side hustles to fund licensure.**

The Project Management Mindset

Licensure is not an event; it's a project.

- **Programming Phase**: Understand all costs and requirements.
- **Schematic Design**: Build a budget.
- **Design Development**: Choose study materials and timelines.
- **Construction Documents**: Schedule exams.
- **Construction Phase**: Execute.
- **Closeout**: Celebrate licensure and plan next career steps.

Treat your licensure journey with the same precision you bring to your design work.

Final Thoughts

Professional licensure is a milestone worth celebrating — but it's one that demands financial foresight.

Plan for the costs. Budget for the journey. Build in flexibility for the inevitable surprises.

You are more capable than you think — and you're building a future you can be proud of.

Financial planning isn't about being perfect — it's about laying the groundwork and refining it over time.

The smartest architects don't just design beautiful buildings — they design sustainable lives.

Keep reviewing and updating your financial blueprint as your career progresses.

Let's continue building something lasting.

Part II: The Launch — First Job, First Paycheck

Graduation marks the end of formal education, but it's only the beginning of your financial journey. *Part II: The Launch – First Job, First Paycheck* guides you through one of the most critical transitions in your career — moving from student to practicing professional.

This section provides the blueprint for navigating your first job offer with confidence. You'll learn how to decode salary and benefits packages, understand your paycheck beyond the surface numbers, and create a financial plan that aligns with your new income and evolving responsibilities. We'll break down essential topics such as evaluating offer letters, setting up the right bank accounts for direct deposit, and developing a strategy to balance loan repayment with saving and investing.

You'll also tackle real-world decisions architects face early in their careers: Should you rent or buy? How aggressively should you pay down student debt? Is it too early to start saving for retirement (spoiler: it's not)?

By applying the same project management mindset you use for architecture to your finances — defining scope, allocating resources, and planning for contingencies — you'll avoid common pitfalls and set the foundation for a resilient, sustainable financial life.

Part II isn't just about managing your first paycheck — it's about building systems and habits that will serve you through every phase of your career. This is where your financial foundation transforms into a true architectural structure — durable, intentional, and ready to support the life you're designing.

Chapter 7: Evaluating Your First Offer Letter

First Impressions: The Start of Your Financial Blueprint

Your first offer letter is more than just a job offer — it's the foundation of your professional and financial future. As an aspiring architect, this document holds critical details that will impact not only your first year out of school but the trajectory of your entire career.

Accepting an offer without fully understanding its terms is like breaking ground on a project without reviewing the construction documents. It can lead to costly mistakes and setbacks. Taking a thoughtful, structured approach to evaluating your first offer letter ensures you start your professional journey with clarity, confidence, and control.

Salary Benchmarks in Architecture: What They Tell You (and What They Don't)

Architecture is a passion-driven field, but passion alone doesn't pay the bills. Salary transparency in architecture has improved, but wide variations remain based on geography, firm size, and market conditions.

Understanding the Numbers

Average Salaries

- Entry-level architectural interns or designers typically earn between **$50,000 and $65,000** per year.
- Larger firms in major cities (New York, San Francisco, Boston) often offer higher salaries but come with higher costs of living.
- Smaller firms or those in lower-cost-of-living areas might offer starting salaries closer to **$45,000**.

Factors Influencing Salary

- **Geography**: Urban vs. rural, high-cost vs. low-cost areas.
- **Firm Size**: Large corporate firms often pay more but may come with less flexibility.
- **Experience**: Internships, co-ops, and portfolio strength.
- **Licensure Progress**: Closer to being licensed? Higher offers.

What Salary Numbers Don't Tell You

A salary number alone doesn't reflect:

- **Overtime Expectations**: Are you salaried exempt (no overtime) or hourly (eligible for overtime)?
- **Bonus Structures**: Some firms offer year-end bonuses or profit sharing.
- **Raises and Promotions**: Is there a clear path and timeline for salary increases?

Action Step

Research salary data through resources like the AIA Compensation Report, Glassdoor, and LinkedIn Salary Insights.

Decoding the Offer Letter

1. Base Salary

This is the foundation of your compensation package. Confirm:

- Amount.
- Pay schedule (bi-weekly, monthly).
- Salary review timelines.

2. Benefits Package

Benefits can add 25-40% to the value of your salary, yet many candidates overlook them.

401(k) or Retirement Plans

What to Look For

- **Employer Match**: Common matches are 3%-6%. A match is essentially free money.
- **Vesting Schedule**: How long you need to stay with the firm to own the employer's contributions.
- **Investment Options**: Are the plan's investment choices diversified and low-cost?

Example

- Base Salary: $55,000
- 401(k) match: 4% = $2,200 per year

Action Step

Contribute at least enough to capture the full match immediately.

Health Insurance

Key Questions

- **Premiums**: How much do you pay monthly?
- **Coverage**: What does the insurance cover? Deductibles, co-pays, out-of-pocket maximums?
- **Network**: Are your preferred doctors in-network?

Types

- **PPO**: Higher premiums, more flexibility.
- **HMO**: Lower premiums, less flexibility.

Additional Coverage

- **Dental and Vision**: Often separate add-ons.
- **Life and Disability Insurance**: Some firms offer basic coverage at no cost.

Paid Time Off (PTO)

What's Standard

- 10-15 days vacation.
- 5-10 sick days.
- Paid holidays.

Other Leave

- **Parental Leave**: Varies widely.
- **Sabbaticals**: Some firms offer extended leave after a set number of years.

Licensure Reimbursement

Many firms encourage licensure and will:

- Reimburse ARE exam fees.
- Pay for study materials.
- Provide paid time off to sit for exams.

Licensure support can be worth several thousand dollars.

Action Step

Confirm whether licensure reimbursement is included in writing.

Professional Development

Look for:

- Continuing education support.
- Conference attendance.
- Software training.

Firms investing in your growth signal a commitment to your long-term development.

Bonuses and Profit Sharing

Some firms offer bonuses based on:

- Personal performance.
- Firm-wide profitability.

Understand how bonuses are calculated and if they are guaranteed or discretionary.

Other Perks

Modern firms may offer:

- Wellness programs.
- Commuter benefits.
- Gym memberships.
- Flexible working hours or remote work options.

Evaluating the Whole Package

Calculate Total Compensation

Base Salary + 401(k) Match + Health Benefits + PTO Value + Licensure Support + Bonuses = Total Compensation

Example

- Base Salary: $55,000
- 401(k) Match: $2,200
- Health Insurance Premium Savings: $3,000
- PTO Value (15 days): $3,200
- Licensure Support: $1,500
- Bonus Potential: $2,500

Total Compensation: ~$67,400

Red Flags to Watch For

- No 401(k) plan.
- No licensure support.
- Unclear bonus structures.
- High health insurance premiums.
- Vague promises instead of written commitments.

Action Step

Ask for a detailed breakdown of benefits before accepting the offer.

Pros and Cons of First Offers

Pros

- Entry into the profession.
- Professional growth opportunities.
- Financial independence.

Cons

- Entry-level salaries are modest.
- Benefits can vary significantly.

Real-World Scenario

Imagine this:

You have two offers.

- Offer A: $60,000 salary, no 401(k) match, high health insurance costs.
- Offer B: $55,000 salary, 5% 401(k) match, full health coverage, licensure reimbursement.

On the surface, Offer A pays more, but Offer B's benefits add significant value and reduce your out-of-pocket costs.

With a careful analysis, you choose Offer B, setting yourself up for stronger long-term growth and stability.

Negotiating Your Offer

Negotiation is standard. Key areas to negotiate:

- Base salary.
- Signing bonus.
- Additional PTO.
- Remote work flexibility.
- Licensure support if not offered.

Always express enthusiasm and professionalism.

Action Step

Prepare a counteroffer supported by market research and your unique qualifications.

Final Thoughts

Evaluating your first offer letter is one of the most important financial decisions you will make early in your career. Treat it with the same rigor you would apply to a new design project — careful analysis, thoughtful questioning, and structured decision-making.

You are more capable than you think — and you're building a future you can be proud of.

Financial planning isn't about being perfect — it's about laying the groundwork and refining it over time.

The smartest architects don't just design beautiful buildings — they design sustainable lives.

Keep reviewing and updating your financial blueprint as your career progresses.

Let's continue building something lasting.

Chapter 8: Your First Paycheck — Understanding Deductions

Introduction: First Paycheck Excitement Meets Reality

There's a unique thrill when you receive your first paycheck as a professional architect. After years of study, sleepless nights in studio, and countless models and crits, the reward feels well-earned. However, the number you see in your offer letter and the amount deposited into your checking account are not the same — and for many, the first encounter with payroll deductions can be jarring.

Understanding where your money goes — taxes, benefits, and savings — is crucial. If your salary is the blueprint, your deductions are the construction details. And just as no building can stand without careful attention to those details, no financial life can thrive without a clear grasp of what's happening behind your paycheck.

Taxes: The Unavoidable Deduction

Taxes are the first major line item reducing your gross salary to a smaller net paycheck.

Federal Taxes

What They Are

The federal government taxes your income to fund public services — infrastructure, defense, education, and more.

How They Work

- **Progressive System**: Higher earners pay a higher percentage.
- **Tax Brackets**: Your income is taxed in tiers.

Marginal vs. Effective Tax Rate

- **Marginal Rate**: The rate on your last dollar earned.
- **Effective Rate**: The average rate you pay on all income.

State Taxes

Varies by State

- Some states (Texas, Florida) have no income tax.
- Others (California, New York) have high state income taxes.

Withholding

Your employer deducts estimated state taxes each paycheck.

FICA: Social Security and Medicare

What They Are

- **Social Security**: Funds retirement benefits.
- **Medicare**: Funds health coverage for retirees.

Rates

- **Social Security**: 6.2% of your wages.
- **Medicare**: 1.45% of your wages.

Your employer matches these contributions.

Other Taxes

- **Local Taxes**: Some cities charge additional income taxes.
- **Additional Medicare Tax**: High earners pay an extra 0.9%.

Action Step

Check your pay stub for:

- Federal withholding.
- State withholding.
- Social Security.
- Medicare.

Benefits Deductions: Pre-Tax vs. Post-Tax

Understanding how your benefits are deducted impacts your take-home pay and tax liability.

Pre-Tax Deductions

What They Include

- Health insurance premiums.
- Dental and vision insurance.
- Retirement contributions (traditional 401(k)).
- Health Savings Accounts (HSA) or Flexible Spending Accounts (FSA).

Why They Matter

Pre-tax deductions lower your taxable income, reducing the taxes you owe.

Example

- Gross Salary: $55,000
- 401(k) Contribution (5%): $2,750 pre-tax
- New taxable income: $52,250

Post-Tax Deductions

What They Include

- Roth 401(k) contributions.
- Life and disability insurance premiums (sometimes).
- Certain union dues.

Why They Matter

Post-tax contributions are made after taxes are withheld. They don't reduce taxable income but can offer other benefits (e.g., tax-free withdrawals from Roth accounts).

Understanding Your Pay Stub

Your pay stub breaks down:

- **Gross Pay**: Your salary before deductions.
- **Pre-Tax Deductions**: Contributions that reduce taxable income.
- **Tax Withholdings**: Federal, state, and FICA.
- **Post-Tax Deductions**: Deductions after taxes.
- **Net Pay**: Your take-home amount.

Action Step

Request a sample pay stub from HR before your first paycheck to familiarize yourself.

Planning for Automatic Savings

Your paycheck is more than spending money; it's your first tool for wealth building.

401(k) Contributions

Employer-Sponsored Retirement Plans

- Many firms offer a 401(k) with a matching contribution.
- Contributions are typically deducted pre-tax.

How Much to Contribute

- At minimum, contribute enough to get the full employer match.
- Ideal starting point: 10%-15% of your salary.

Health Savings Account (HSA)

If you have a high-deductible health plan (HDHP), you can contribute to an HSA.

- Pre-tax contributions.
- Funds roll over year to year.
- Can be used for current and future medical expenses.

Action Step

Max out HSA contributions if possible.

Emergency Fund Contributions

Set up automatic transfers from your checking account to a high-yield savings account.

- Start with $50-$100 per paycheck.
- Goal: 3-6 months' worth of living expenses.

Real-World Scenario

Imagine this:

- Gross salary: $55,000/year.
- Monthly gross pay: ~$4,583.

Deductions:

- 401(k) Contribution (5%): -$229
- Health Insurance Premium: -$150
- Federal Taxes: -$550

- State Taxes: -$200
- FICA (Social Security + Medicare): -$350

Net Pay: ~$3,104
Automatic Transfers:

- Emergency Fund: $100
- Roth IRA Contribution: $200

Spendable Income: ~$2,804
Without planning:

- You wonder why your checking account never grows.

With planning:

- You're saving for retirement and emergencies without thinking about it.

Pros and Cons of Pre-Tax vs. Post-Tax Contributions

Pre-Tax

Pros:

- Lowers taxable income.
- Immediate tax savings.

Cons:

- Taxes owed upon withdrawal.

Post-Tax

Pros:

- Tax-free withdrawals in retirement.

Cons:

- No immediate tax benefit.

Key Considerations

- Review your W-4 form to adjust federal withholding.
- Adjust benefits during open enrollment annually.
- Increase retirement contributions when you get raises.

Action Steps to Start

1. **Request a Sample Pay Stub**: Understand deductions before payday.
2. **Elect Retirement Contributions**: Aim for at least the employer match.
3. **Set Up HSA or FSA Contributions**: Maximize pre-tax savings.
4. **Open a High-Yield Savings Account**: Automate emergency fund contributions.
5. **Review Benefits Annually**: Adjust as needed based on life changes.

The Project Management Mindset

Treat your paycheck like a construction project.

- **Pre-Design**: Know your total gross salary.
- **Schematic Design**: Understand deductions.
- **Design Development**: Plan savings and investments.

- **Construction Documents**: Set up automations.
- **Construction Phase**: Execute your financial plan.
- **Closeout**: Review and adjust regularly.

Final Thoughts

Your paycheck is more than a paycheck — it's your financial foundation.

Understand where your money goes. Make deductions work for you, not against you. And set up systems to build wealth automatically, just as you would lay a foundation designed to last.

You are more capable than you think — and you're building a future you can be proud of.

Financial planning isn't about being perfect — it's about laying the groundwork and refining it over time.

The smartest architects don't just design beautiful buildings — they design sustainable lives.

Keep reviewing and updating your financial blueprint as your career progresses.

Let's continue building something lasting.

Chapter 9: Renting vs Buying Early in Your Career

Introduction: The Crossroads of Early Financial Decisions

As a new architect, standing at the threshold of your professional life, you're confronted with one of the biggest financial decisions you'll ever make: should you rent or buy your home?

The allure of homeownership is powerful. For many, it's seen as a symbol of adulthood, stability, and success. But is buying property early in your career the smart move? Or does it make more sense to rent, build financial flexibility, and keep your options open?

Just as every site has its unique challenges and opportunities, so too does your financial landscape. Let's walk through the architecture of this decision, breaking it down brick by brick.

Should an Architect Buy Property Early?

Understanding the Traditional Narrative

Homeownership has long been portrayed as a financial rite of passage. "Stop throwing money away on rent," they say. "Build equity," they insist.

But architecture careers, especially early on, don't always fit neatly into that narrative.

The Realities of Early Career Architecture

- **Modest Starting Salaries**: First-year architects typically earn $50,000 to $65,000.
- **Student Loan Debt**: Many architects graduate with significant debt.
- **Career Mobility**: Early career moves are common to gain diverse experience.
- **Licensure Process**: Time and money are needed for exams and professional development.

Committing to a mortgage can limit your flexibility at a time when adaptability is crucial.

Homeownership Myths and Realities for Young Professionals

Myth 1: "Renting Is Throwing Money Away"

The Reality

Renting provides flexibility and limits your liability.

- No property taxes.
- No maintenance costs.
- No risk of market downturns.

Renting is paying for the **use** of a home without the long-term obligations that come with ownership.

Action Step

Calculate how much "throwing away" you're really doing compared to ownership costs.

Myth 2: "Real Estate Always Appreciates"

The Reality

Markets fluctuate.

- Property values can drop.
- Selling a home can take months and cost 6-10% in fees.
- Economic downturns can leave homeowners "underwater" (owing more than the home is worth).

Appreciation is not guaranteed.

Myth 3: "A Mortgage Is Cheaper Than Rent"

The Reality

Mortgage payments are just the beginning.
Ownership costs include:

- Property taxes.
- Homeowners insurance.
- Maintenance and repairs (1%-3% of home value annually).
- HOA fees (if applicable).

Myth 4: "Buying Young Means You'll Be Mortgage-Free Sooner"

The Reality

Early buying can lock you into a location or home that doesn't fit your future life or career.

Moving later could mean selling costs, transaction fees, and potential losses.

Pros and Cons of Renting

Pros

- Flexibility to relocate.
- Lower upfront costs (security deposit vs. down payment).
- Predictable monthly expenses.
- No maintenance worries.

Cons

- No equity buildup.
- Subject to rent increases.
- Limited customization.

Pros and Cons of Buying

Pros

- Potential for equity growth.
- Tax deductions on mortgage interest.
- Stability and control.

Cons

- High upfront costs (down payment, closing costs).
- Ongoing maintenance expenses.
- Potential for depreciation.
- Limits on career mobility.

Action Steps for Decision-Making

Step 1: Run the Numbers

Use a rent vs. buy calculator.

- Factor in:
- Rent cost.
- Home price.
- Down payment.
- Interest rate.
- Taxes and insurance.
- Maintenance.
- Projected appreciation.

Step 2: Consider Your Career Trajectory

- Are you planning to stay in one place for at least 5-7 years?
- Is your firm stable?
- Will you pursue licensure or grad school elsewhere?

Step 3: Assess Financial Readiness

You should have:

- A 20% down payment to avoid PMI (private mortgage insurance).

- 3-6 months' worth of emergency savings.
- Low to manageable debt levels.

Action Step

Delay buying until you meet these benchmarks.

Step 4: Evaluate Lifestyle Factors

- Commute preferences.
- Desire for urban vs. suburban living.
- Willingness to maintain property.

Real-World Scenario

Imagine this:

- Salary: $58,000
- Monthly rent: $1,200
- Comparable home price: $250,000
- 20% down: $50,000

After adding in taxes, insurance, maintenance, and opportunity costs (what you could have done with the $50,000), buying is more expensive monthly unless you stay put for 7+ years.

Without careful analysis:

- You buy too early.
- Career growth requires relocation.
- You face selling costs and possible financial loss.

With careful analysis:

- You rent while advancing in your career.
- You save aggressively.
- You buy when your foundation is stronger.

The "Starter Home" Trap

Many young professionals buy "starter homes" thinking they'll trade up in a few years.

Hidden Costs

- Selling costs (agent commissions, closing costs).
- Moving expenses.
- Time and emotional energy.

Starter homes can be costly stepping stones if not planned carefully.

The Architecture-Specific Lens

Your Skills Create Unique Risks and Opportunities

- **Design Bias**: You'll be tempted to remodel or "fix" homes, draining time and money.
- **Job Mobility**: Early career architects often change firms or cities.
- **Entrepreneurship**: If you want to open your own practice, liquidity (cash) is more important than home equity.

Action Step

Delay major property commitments until you have career clarity.

The Financial Blueprint for Early Career Architects

Renting Wisely

- Negotiate lease terms.
- Look for rent-stabilized units.
- Keep housing costs below 30% of your gross income.

Preparing to Buy

- Build an emergency fund.
- Save for a 20% down payment.
- Improve credit scores for better mortgage rates.
- Understand all ownership costs.

Homeownership Timeline

1. 0-5 Years Post-Graduation

- Focus on career growth.
- Build savings.
- Rent for flexibility.

1. 5-10 Years Post-Graduation

- Assess career stability.
- Buy only if you plan to stay for 7+ years.

1. 10+ Years Post-Graduation

- Homeownership becomes a more logical next step.

Key Metrics to Watch

- **Rent-to-Income Ratio**: Aim for rent below 30% of gross monthly income.
- **Debt-to-Income Ratio**: Lenders prefer under 36%.
- **Savings Rate**: Target 20%+ of income toward savings and investments.

Final Thoughts

Renting vs. buying is not a moral decision; it's a financial strategy. As an architect, you've been trained to think in terms of systems, durability, and long-term outcomes. Apply the same logic to your financial life.

Rent when it provides freedom and financial flexibility. Buy when your career, finances, and life goals are ready to support the structure of ownership.

You are more capable than you think — and you're building a future you can be proud of.

Financial planning isn't about being perfect — it's about laying the groundwork and refining it over time.

The smartest architects don't just design beautiful buildings — they design sustainable lives.

Keep reviewing and updating your financial blueprint as your life evolves.

Let's continue building something lasting.

Chapter 10: Student Loan Repayment Begins

Introduction: Welcome to Repayment

For many young architects, graduating from school feels like crossing a finish line. But as the confetti settles, reality sets in: student loan repayment begins.

Student loans are a fact of life for many in the profession. Architectural education is long and expensive, and balancing loan repayment with starting salaries can be challenging. Yet, with the right repayment plan and a few strategic moves, managing your student debt doesn't have to overwhelm your budget or your life.

This chapter is your blueprint for approaching repayment with confidence and clarity.

Choosing the Right Repayment Plan

Student loans aren't one-size-fits-all. Choosing the right repayment plan is critical to ensure your monthly payments are manageable and align with your broader financial goals.

Federal Student Loan Repayment Plans

Federal student loans offer multiple repayment plans.

Standard Repayment Plan

Details

- Fixed monthly payments.
- Term: 10 years.

Pros

- Pay less interest over the life of the loan.
- Loan paid off faster.

Cons

- Higher monthly payments.

Best For

Graduates who can afford higher monthly payments and want to minimize interest costs.

Graduated Repayment Plan

Details

- Payments start lower and increase every two years.
- Term: 10 years.

Pros

- Lower payments early when salary is lower.

Cons

- Pay more interest over time.

Best For

Graduates who expect significant salary growth.

Extended Repayment Plan

Details

- Fixed or graduated payments.
- Term: Up to 25 years.

Pros

- Lower monthly payments.

Cons

- Pay significantly more interest over time.

Best For

Graduates with high loan balances who need to reduce monthly expenses.

Income-Driven Repayment (IDR) Plans

Includes:

- Income-Based Repayment (IBR).
- Pay As You Earn (PAYE).
- Revised Pay As You Earn (REPAYE).
- Income-Contingent Repayment (ICR).

Details

- Payments based on discretionary income.
- Loan forgiveness after 20-25 years.

Pros

- Payments adjust with income.
- Potential for forgiveness.

Cons

- Interest may capitalize.
- Higher total repayment over time.

Best For

Graduates with lower starting salaries or those pursuing Public Service Loan Forgiveness (PSLF).

Public Service Loan Forgiveness (PSLF)

Details

- Requires 120 qualifying payments under an IDR plan.
- Work must be full-time for a qualifying employer (government or non-profit).

Pros

- Tax-free loan forgiveness.

Cons

- Strict documentation requirements.
- Must remain in qualifying employment.

Best For

Architects working for non-profits, government agencies, or academic institutions.

Private Loan Repayment

Private loans typically have fewer repayment options.

Tips

- Ask your lender about interest rate reductions for automatic payments.
- Consider refinancing if you have strong credit and a stable income.

Key Considerations When Choosing a Plan

- Current salary and expenses.
- Projected salary growth.
- Total loan balance.
- Career plans (e.g., public vs. private sector).

Strategies for Prepayment Without Overwhelming Your Budget

Paying extra toward your loans can save thousands in interest. But how do you do it without sacrificing other financial goals?

Understand Interest Accrual

Interest accrues daily based on your loan balance.

- Paying early in the month can reduce interest.
- Extra payments should be directed toward principal.

Start Small

Even an extra $50 per month can:

- Reduce your principal.
- Lower your total interest paid.

Use Windfalls Wisely

- Tax refunds.
- Work bonuses.
- Freelance income.

Apply these to loans rather than lifestyle inflation.

Automate Extra Payments

- Set up automatic extra payments each month.
- Small amounts add up without conscious effort.

Prioritize High-Interest Loans

If you have multiple loans:

- Focus extra payments on the highest-interest loan (avalanche method).
- Alternatively, pay off the smallest loan first for psychological wins (snowball method).

Avoid These Mistakes

- Making extra payments without specifying they go to principal.
- Paying extra before building an emergency fund.
- Sacrificing retirement contributions for loan prepayment.

Real-World Scenario

Imagine this:

- Student loan balance: $70,000
- Average interest rate: 5%
- Standard monthly payment: ~$742

If you pay an extra $100 per month:

- Loan payoff reduces by about 2 years.
- Save ~$3,700 in interest.

Without a plan:

- Loans linger for a decade.
- You pay tens of thousands in interest.

With a plan:

- Loans are paid off sooner.
- You free up cash flow for investing and building wealth.

Pros and Cons of Prepayment

Pros

- Save money on interest.
- Achieve debt freedom sooner.
- Improve your debt-to-income ratio.

Cons

- May delay investing.
- Less liquidity if you overcommit cash.

Action Steps to Begin

1. **Inventory Your Loans**: Federal vs. private, interest rates, balances.
2. **Choose a Repayment Plan**: Based on income, goals, and career path.
3. **Set a Prepayment Goal**: Extra $50-$200 per month.
4. **Automate Payments**: Ensure consistency.
5. **Reassess Annually**: Adjust as salary and life circumstances change.

The Project Management Mindset

Approach loan repayment like a phased construction project.

- **Schematic Design**: Understand your loan details.
- **Design Development**: Choose the best repayment plan.
- **Construction Documents**: Set payment schedules and goals.
- **Construction Phase**: Execute consistently.
- **Closeout**: Celebrate milestones (paying off first loan, reducing principal by half).

Final Thoughts

Student loans can feel overwhelming, but they don't have to define your financial future.

Choose the right repayment plan. Make strategic prepayments without sacrificing your other goals. Remember, loans are temporary — but the financial habits you build now will last a lifetime.

You are more capable than you think — and you're building a future you can be proud of.

Financial planning isn't about being perfect — it's about laying the groundwork and refining it over time.

The smartest architects don't just design beautiful buildings — they design sustainable lives.

Keep reviewing and updating your financial blueprint as your life evolves.

Let's continue building something lasting.

Chapter 11: Starting Your Retirement Savings Early

Introduction: The Foundation for Long-Term Wealth

As an architect, you understand that the strongest, most durable structures are built on foundations laid early, with careful planning and precision. Your financial future works exactly the same way. Starting your retirement savings early in your career is not about depriving yourself today — it's about constructing a solid base that can support the life you want decades down the road.

When you're balancing student loans, rent, and modest starting salaries, retirement might seem like a distant, abstract concept. But the reality is this: the earlier you start saving, even small amounts, the greater your financial freedom later. Time is your most powerful asset.

401(k), 403(b), and IRA Options: Building Your Financial Structure

There are several retirement savings vehicles available to young architects. Choosing the right one, or combination, is a matter of understanding the tools and how they work.

401(k) Plans

What It Is

A 401(k) is an employer-sponsored retirement savings plan.

Key Features

- **Pre-Tax Contributions**: Reduces your taxable income today.
- **Employer Match**: Many employers match a percentage of your contributions.
- **Contribution Limits**: $23,000/year (as of 2025).

Why It Matters

Employer matching contributions are essentially free money. Not contributing at least enough to get the full match is like refusing part of your salary.

Vesting Schedules

Some employers require you to stay for a certain number of years before you "own" all the matching contributions.

Action Step

Contribute at least enough to get the full employer match.

403(b) Plans

What It Is

A 403(b) plan is similar to a 401(k) but offered by non-profits and public sector employers (e.g., universities, government agencies).

Key Features

- Pre-tax contributions.
- Employer match (varies).
- Same contribution limits as 401(k).

IRA Options

When a 401(k) isn't available, or if you want to save additional money, IRAs (Individual Retirement Accounts) are powerful tools.

Traditional IRA

What It Is

An individual account where contributions may be tax-deductible.

Key Features

- Contributions may reduce taxable income (if you meet income limits).
- Taxes deferred until withdrawal.
- Contribution Limit: $7,000/year (as of 2025).

Roth IRA

What It Is

An individual account where contributions are made with after-tax dollars.

Key Features

- Contributions are not tax-deductible.
- Earnings grow tax-free.
- Withdrawals are tax-free in retirement.
- Income limits apply.

Roth vs. Traditional IRAs for Young Architects

Choosing between a Roth and Traditional IRA comes down to a few key factors.

Roth IRA Advantages

- You're likely in a lower tax bracket now than you will be later.
- Contributions (not earnings) can be withdrawn anytime without penalty.
- Tax-free income in retirement.

Traditional IRA Advantages

- Immediate tax deduction (if eligible).
- Lowers taxable income today.

Key Considerations

Your Current vs. Future Tax Bracket

- Early-career architects typically have lower incomes.
- Tax-free growth in a Roth IRA can be more valuable over time.

Flexibility

- Roth IRAs allow for more flexible withdrawals.

Employer Plans

- Maximize employer 401(k) match first.
- Then contribute to a Roth IRA if eligible.

Real-World Scenario

Imagine this:

- Salary: $58,000/year.
- 401(k) Match: 4%.

You contribute 4% ($2,320) to get the full match.
Then, you open a Roth IRA and contribute $5,000/year.
Over 30 years:

- 401(k) grows with pre-tax contributions.
- Roth IRA grows tax-free.

Without early saving:

- You scramble in your 40s and 50s to "catch up."

With early saving:

- Compounding works in your favor.
- Small contributions today turn into substantial wealth tomorrow.

Compounding: The Architect's Secret Weapon

The earlier you start saving, the more you benefit from compounding — earning returns on your past returns.

Example:

- Save $5,000/year starting at age 25.
- Stop saving at 35.
- Let it grow at 7% annual return.

At 65, you'd have ~$500,000 without adding another dime after 35.

Starting 10 years later, you'd need to save over $10,000/year to reach the same result.

Automating Your Retirement Savings

Make saving effortless:

- Set up automatic payroll deductions to 401(k).
- Set up automatic transfers to IRAs.

Treat savings like a non-negotiable bill.

Pros and Cons of Starting Early

Pros

- More time for compounding.
- Smaller monthly contributions required.
- Reduces future financial stress.

Cons

- Harder when starting salaries are modest.
- Competing financial priorities (student loans, rent).

Strategies for Success

1. **Prioritize the Employer Match**: Never leave free money on the table.
2. **Max Out Roth IRA If Possible**: After the match, Roth IRAs are a great next step.
3. **Increase Contributions Over Time**: Boost your savings rate with each raise.
4. **Don't Raid Your Accounts**: Early withdrawals trigger penalties and taxes.
5. **Stay the Course**: Market ups and downs are normal — keep contributing.

Key Metrics to Watch

- **Savings Rate**: Aim for 15% of gross income (combined across all accounts).
- **Account Balances**: Track growth annually.
- **Investment Fees**: Opt for low-cost index funds.

Real-World Complications

- Career changes may mean rolling over old 401(k)s.
- Early-career architects often relocate — keep retirement savings portable.
- Self-employment requires setting up solo 401(k)s or SEP IRAs.

Action Step

Understand the retirement plan options offered by new employers before accepting offers.

Architect-Specific Considerations

- Many architects work for small firms with limited benefits.
- Freelance or self-employed architects need to create their own retirement plans.
- Architecture careers can be long — many work well into their 60s and 70s — but planning early gives the option to retire when you want, not when you have to.

The Project Management Mindset

Treat retirement planning like designing a major project.

- **Programming Phase**: Understand your goals and resources.
- **Schematic Design**: Set savings targets.
- **Design Development**: Choose account types.
- **Construction Documents**: Automate contributions.
- **Construction Phase**: Stay consistent.
- **Closeout**: Adjust as life evolves.

Final Thoughts

Starting your retirement savings early is one of the most powerful financial moves you can make.

The key isn't how much you start with — it's that you start. Every dollar saved today builds the scaffolding for a future of financial independence.

You are more capable than you think — and you're building a future you can be proud of.

Financial planning isn't about being perfect — it's about laying the groundwork and refining it over time.

The smartest architects don't just design beautiful buildings — they design sustainable lives.

Keep reviewing and updating your financial blueprint as your career progresses.

Let's continue building something lasting.

Chapter 12: Setting a Realistic Early Career Budget

Introduction: The Blueprint for Financial Stability

Graduating into the architecture profession is a moment of well-earned pride. After years of study, you're finally earning a paycheck and stepping into your career. But the early years of working life are also some of the most critical for setting the tone of your financial future.

Just as a well-conceived design project starts with a realistic budget, so too must your financial life. An early career budget isn't just about paying bills; it's about creating a structure that supports your long-term goals. It balances living well now with planning for the future. It guards against lifestyle creep. It lays the foundation for resilience when life's inevitable surprises occur.

Let's design a budget that does what every good structure should do: stand the test of time.

Balancing Lifestyle Creep and Studio Culture

Understanding Lifestyle Creep

Lifestyle creep happens when your spending increases as your income rises. It's tempting — and in architecture, where creative environments and studio culture often blend work and life, it's easy to justify.

You finish a big project. You get a raise. You celebrate with a more expensive apartment or a new car. Suddenly, you're locked into higher monthly expenses.

Why Architects Are Vulnerable

- **Studio Culture**: Architecture firms often blur the line between work and life. Dinners, happy hours, late nights at the office.
- **Aesthetic Sensibility**: You're trained to appreciate design, quality, and beauty — which can translate into expensive taste.
- **Slow Income Growth**: Raises in architecture often lag behind other professions.

Guardrails Against Lifestyle Creep

1. Set a Lifestyle Baseline

Determine what level of living makes you comfortable, not what others expect.

2. Delay Big Upgrades

Give yourself a one-year cooling-off period before upgrading your car, apartment, or wardrobe.

3. Automate Savings

Channel raises and bonuses into savings before you even see them.

4. Stay Connected to Your Goals

Remember: early sacrifices yield major long-term benefits.

Building an Emergency Fund

What Is an Emergency Fund?

An emergency fund is cash set aside to cover unexpected expenses without resorting to debt.

Examples:

- Medical emergencies.
- Car repairs.
- Job loss.

How Much Do You Need?

- **Minimum**: 3 months' worth of living expenses.
- **Ideal**: 6 months' worth.

Living expenses include:

- Rent.
- Utilities.
- Insurance.
- Food.
- Transportation.

Where to Keep It

- High-yield savings account.
- Separate from your daily checking account.
- Accessible but not too easy to dip into.

Building It Slowly

Start small:

- $25/week = $1,300/year.
- Tax refunds, bonuses, and freelance income can accelerate growth.

Action Step

Automate weekly or biweekly transfers.

The Components of a Realistic Early Career Budget

Income

Know your net income — what's left after taxes and deductions.
If you earn $55,000 annually:

- Estimated take-home (after taxes and deductions): ~$3,200/month.

Fixed Expenses

These are non-negotiable monthly costs:

- Rent/mortgage.
- Utilities.
- Loan payments.

- Insurance premiums.

Rule of Thumb

- Housing: <30% of gross monthly income.

Variable Expenses

Costs that change month to month:

- Groceries.
- Dining out.
- Entertainment.
- Travel.

Savings and Investments

"Pay yourself first."

- 401(k) or 403(b) contributions.
- Roth IRA contributions.
- Emergency fund.

Target Savings Rate

- Aim to save 20% of gross income.

Debt Payments

If you have student loans or credit card debt:

- Factor minimum payments into your budget.
- Try to pay extra on high-interest debt.

Real-World Scenario

Imagine this:

- Salary: $58,000.
- Take-home: ~$3,400/month.

Monthly Budget:

- Rent: $1,000.
- Utilities: $150.
- Transportation: $200.
- Food: $400.
- Loan Payment: $350.
- Insurance: $100.
- Emergency Fund: $150.
- 401(k): $250.
- Roth IRA: $200.
- Entertainment: $150.
- Travel: $150.
- Miscellaneous: $300.

Total: ~$3,300.
This leaves a buffer for unexpected costs.

Pros and Cons of Early Career Budgeting

Pros

- Reduces financial stress.
- Builds savings early.
- Prevents debt.

Cons

- Requires discipline.
- May feel restrictive early on.

Common Budget Pitfalls to Avoid

- **Underestimating variable expenses**.
- **Forgetting irregular expenses** (annual fees, gifts).
- **Overcommitting to housing**.
- **Failing to adjust over time**.

Action Step

Review and revise your budget every 3-6 months.

Budgeting Tools and Apps

- **YNAB (You Need a Budget)**: Great for zero-based budgeting.
- **Mint**: Good for tracking.
- **Personal Capital**: Best for investment tracking.

Choose the one that matches your mindset.

Architect-Specific Considerations

- **Licensure Costs**: Budget for ARE exams, study materials, and fees.
- **Professional Memberships**: AIA dues, NCARB fees.
- **Continuing Education**: Conferences, courses.

These professional expenses are investments in your career but need to be planned for.

Strategies for Staying on Budget

1. Set Up "Sinking Funds"

Save monthly for irregular large expenses like:

- Annual professional dues.
- Travel.
- Gifts.

2. Embrace "No-Spend" Days

Have days where you intentionally don't spend money.

3. Use Cash for Discretionary Spending

Withdraw your entertainment or dining budget in cash to limit overspending.

The Project Management Mindset

Think of your budget as your personal project.

- **Programming**: Identify income and expenses.
- **Schematic Design**: Sketch your budget.
- **Design Development**: Refine your spending.
- **Construction Documents**: Automate savings and payments.
- **Construction Phase**: Execute monthly.
- **Closeout**: Review and adjust quarterly.

Final Thoughts

A realistic early career budget isn't about restriction; it's about intention. It's about ensuring that your spending reflects your values and supports your goals.

Budgeting gives you control. It allows you to build the life you're designing for yourself — not just professionally, but personally.

You are more capable than you think — and you're building a future you can be proud of.

Financial planning isn't about being perfect — it's about laying the groundwork and refining it over time.

The smartest architects don't just design beautiful buildings — they design sustainable lives.

Keep reviewing and updating your financial blueprint as your career evolves.

Let's continue building something lasting.

Part III: Growth Years — Mid-Career Moves and Money

As you move from early career to mid-career, your financial priorities shift — and so should your strategy. *Part III: Growth Years — Mid-Career Moves and Money* addresses the evolving financial landscape architects face after they've laid the initial groundwork.

This section dives into the realities of career advancement, firm transitions, partnership opportunities, and the growing complexity of your financial life. Whether you're changing firms, stepping into leadership roles, or contemplating licensure in additional states, we explore how to navigate these transitions while continuing to build wealth. We'll unpack everything from optimizing retirement contributions to evaluating equity stakes in firms, from managing increasing family obligations to balancing homeownership decisions with career flexibility.

Mid-career is when lifestyle inflation becomes an even greater risk — and when intentionality matters more than ever. You'll learn how to refine your budget, protect your progress with insurance and estate planning, and leverage your increased income without losing sight of your long-term goals.

Part III is not just about preserving what you've built — it's about accelerating toward the life you envision. With the right financial systems in place, your mid-career years can become your most powerful building phase — not just professionally, but personally and financially.

Chapter 13: Changing Firms or Going Solo

Introduction: Career Crossroads and Financial Impact

Architects reach a point when staying on the same career path no longer aligns with their professional goals or personal aspirations. Whether you're considering a move to a new firm or contemplating launching your own practice, these transitions have major financial implications.

A new job can mean a significant salary increase, better benefits, or a faster track to leadership. Going solo can unlock creativity, autonomy, and financial upside — but it also comes with risk and responsibility.

Like any well-designed project, these career moves demand a clear plan. Let's walk through how to evaluate offers, negotiate wisely, and plan financially for the leap from employee to independent architect or small firm owner.

Evaluating Job Offers and Negotiating Salary Increases

Why Architects Switch Firms

- **Career Growth**: Limited upward mobility at current firm.
- **Compensation**: Below-market salary or benefits.
- **Work-Life Balance**: Unsustainable workloads.
- **Specialization**: Seeking a different project type or niche.
- **Culture**: Misalignment with firm values or leadership.

Understanding your "why" helps you evaluate new opportunities clearly.

Dissecting the Job Offer

1. Base Salary

The most obvious metric, but not the only one.

- **Research**: Compare to AIA Compensation Reports and regional salary surveys.
- **Adjust for Cost of Living**: A $10,000 raise may not stretch far in high-cost cities.

Action Step

Calculate your "real" raise after taxes and cost-of-living adjustments.

2. Bonus Structure

- **Performance Bonuses**: Based on personal or firm performance.
- **Signing Bonuses**: Common for hard-to-fill roles.
- **Profit Sharing**: A share of firm profits.

Clarify if bonuses are guaranteed or discretionary.

3. Retirement Benefits

- **401(k) or 403(b) Plans**: Look for strong employer match.
- **Vesting Schedules**: Understand when employer contributions become yours.

4. Health Insurance

Compare:

- Monthly premiums.
- Deductibles.
- Co-pays.
- Coverage networks.

Better insurance can be worth thousands annually.

5. Licensure Support

- **Exam Fee Reimbursement**.
- **Study Material Reimbursement**.
- **Paid Time Off for Exams**.

These can offset significant out-of-pocket costs.

6. Professional Development

- Continuing education stipends.
- Conference attendance.
- Technology allowances.

7. Paid Time Off (PTO)

- Vacation days.
- Sick days.
- Holidays.
- Parental leave.

Negotiating Salary and Benefits

Preparation

- **Know Your Market Value**: Use multiple sources.
- **Have a Number**: Know your target salary.
- **Consider Total Compensation**: Salary + benefits + bonus.

Negotiation Strategies

- **Be Gracious**: Express appreciation first.
- **Frame It**: Emphasize your value, not your needs.
- **Bundle Requests**: Salary, title, benefits — negotiate as a package.
- **Be Ready to Walk**: Only if you're truly prepared to decline.

Transition Planning

- **Check for Non-Competes**: Are you restricted from working with certain clients?
- **Secure References**: Exit professionally to preserve relationships.
- **Plan Timing**: Consider bonus schedules and retirement vesting dates.

Moving From Employee to Independent Contractor or Small Firm Owner

Why Go Solo?

- **Creative Freedom**.
- **Greater Autonomy**.
- **Higher Potential Earnings**.
- **Control Over Clients and Projects**.

But also:

- **Greater Risk**.
- **Variable Income**.
- **Administrative Burdens**.

Financial Preparation

1. Build a "Firm Launch Fund"

Cash cushion to cover:

- Business setup costs.
- 6-12 months of personal living expenses.
- Initial marketing.
- First-year operating expenses.

Target

$50,000 to $100,000 depending on overhead.

2. Legal and Administrative Setup

- **Entity Formation**: LLC, S-Corp, or Sole Proprietor?
- **Business Bank Accounts**.
- **Contracts and Proposals**.

- **Insurance**: Professional liability, general liability.
- **Licensing**: Firm licenses vary by state.

3. Health Insurance and Benefits

Without an employer, you must source:

- Health insurance.
- Disability insurance.
- Retirement savings plan (SEP IRA, Solo 401(k)).

4. Tax Considerations

- **Quarterly Estimated Taxes**.
- **Self-Employment Tax**.
- **Tax Deductions**: Home office, equipment, travel.

Action Step

Hire a CPA experienced in working with small architecture firms.

5. Client Acquisition

- Networking.
- Referral relationships.
- Online presence (website, LinkedIn).

Understand:

- **Ideal Client Profile**.
- **Pricing Strategy**: Hourly, fixed fee, or percentage of construction cost?

Pros and Cons of Going Solo

Pros

- Creative control.
- Flexible work schedule.
- Unlimited earning potential.

Cons

- Income variability.
- Administrative burdens.
- Risk of client nonpayment.

Real-World Scenario

Imagine this:

- Salary: $95,000/year at a firm.
- Launch solo practice with 2 small residential projects.

First-year income:

- $75,000.
- Business expenses: $20,000.

Net: $55,000.

It's less than your previous salary, but with more growth potential and control.

Without a plan:

- Financial instability.
- Stress.

- Potential early failure.

With a plan:

- Manageable risk.
- Gradual income growth.
- Long-term sustainability.

Action Steps to Prepare

1. **Assess Your Finances**: Can you live lean for 1-2 years?
2. **Develop a Business Plan**.
3. **Create a Portfolio of Work**.
4. **Line Up Initial Clients**.
5. **Consult Professionals**: Lawyer, CPA, insurance broker.

The Project Management Mindset

Treat the transition like a phased project:

- **Programming**: Define your goals.
- **Schematic Design**: Research options.
- **Design Development**: Finalize your strategy.
- **Construction Documents**: Legal and financial setup.
- **Construction Phase**: Launch your firm.
- **Closeout**: Evaluate, iterate, grow.

Final Thoughts

Changing firms or going solo is a major career pivot — one that requires the same careful planning you'd devote to a major building project.

Evaluate offers holistically. Negotiate with confidence. And if you're dreaming of your own firm, build the financial foundation first.

You are more capable than you think — and you're building a future you can be proud of.

Financial planning isn't about being perfect — it's about laying the groundwork and refining it over time.

The smartest architects don't just design beautiful buildings — they design sustainable lives.

Keep reviewing and updating your financial blueprint as your career evolves.

Let's continue building something lasting.

Chapter 14: The Business Side of Architecture

Introduction: Architect as Entrepreneur

For many architects, the idea of running a business can feel daunting. After all, your education focused on design, structure, space — not payroll, taxes, and business entities.

But make no mistake: whether you're freelancing part-time or building a full-fledged firm, understanding the business side is crucial. Without it, even the most talented architects risk financial instability, burnout, or worse, closure.

This chapter will guide you through the financial and administrative architecture of setting up your own practice. Whether you dream of running your own firm or want to freelance on the side, we'll help you lay the right foundation.

How to Set Up a Freelance Practice or Firm: LLC, S-Corp, etc.

Step 1: Choose a Business Structure

Choosing the right legal entity is a fundamental decision. It affects your taxes, liability, and how you can grow.

Sole Proprietorship

What It Is

- Default structure if you do nothing.

Pros

- Simple setup.
- Low cost.

Cons

- No liability protection.
- Business debts = personal debts.

Best For

- Very small, low-risk freelance work.

Limited Liability Company (LLC)

What It Is

- Separates business and personal assets.

Pros

- Liability protection.
- Simple taxation (pass-through).
- Flexible management.

Cons

- Annual filing fees.
- Self-employment tax.

Best For

- Solo architects and small firms.

S-Corporation (S-Corp)

What It Is

- Special tax status for corporations.

Pros

- Liability protection.
- Potential tax savings by splitting salary and distributions.

Cons

- More administrative work.
- Must pay yourself a "reasonable" salary.

Best For

- Firms generating $80,000+ profit per year.

C-Corporation

What It Is

- Standard corporation.

Pros

- Strong liability protection.
- Easier to raise investment capital.

Cons

- Double taxation (corporate + personal).
- High administrative burden.

Best For

- Large firms with multiple shareholders.

Professional Corporation (PC) / Professional LLC (PLLC)

Some states require architects to form a PC or PLLC.

Check State Laws

- States vary on structure requirements for licensed professionals.

Action Step

Consult an attorney familiar with professional firms.

Step 2: Register Your Business

- File with your state.
- Obtain an Employer Identification Number (EIN).
- Open a business bank account.
- Apply for any necessary local business licenses.

Step 3: Insurance

- Professional liability (errors and omissions) insurance.
- General liability insurance.
- Workers' compensation (if you have employees).

Step 4: Contracts and Proposals

Have standard templates for:

- Client proposals.
- Service contracts.
- Change orders.
- Invoices.

Clear contracts protect you legally and financially.

Step 5: Branding and Marketing

- Business name.
- Logo and website.
- Portfolio.
- Social media presence.

Your brand identity should reflect your firm's style and values.

Step 6: Licensure and Continuing Education

- Ensure firm licensure requirements are met.
- Keep up with continuing education credits.
- Understand your state's rules for firm naming and ownership.

Tax Implications and Quarterly Estimated Taxes

Self-Employment Taxes

When you work for yourself, you're responsible for:

- Income tax.
- Self-employment tax (covers Social Security and Medicare).

Self-Employment Tax Rate

- 15.3% (12.4% Social Security + 2.9% Medicare).

Quarterly Estimated Taxes

You must pay taxes as you earn income, not just once a year.

Deadlines

- April 15
- June 15
- September 15
- January 15 (following year)

How to Calculate

- Estimate your total annual income.
- Subtract deductions.
- Apply your tax rate.
- Divide by 4.

Or use:

- IRS Form 1040-ES.
- Online tax calculators.

Action Step

Set up a separate savings account for tax payments.

Deductions and Write-Offs

You can deduct:

- Home office expenses.
- Office rent.

- Equipment and software.
- Internet and phone.
- Professional dues and subscriptions.
- Continuing education.
- Travel and meals (business-related).

Keep detailed records and receipts.

Hiring a CPA

A good CPA can:

- Help you choose the right business structure.
- Set up bookkeeping systems.
- Maximize your deductions.
- Ensure compliance with tax laws.

Look for a CPA experienced with small professional service firms.

Real-World Scenario

Imagine:

- Freelance architect earns $120,000/year.
- After expenses, net income = $100,000.
- Self-employment tax = ~$15,300.
- Federal and state income taxes = ~$20,000.

Without quarterly payments:

- Big tax bill at year-end.

With quarterly payments:

- Smaller, manageable payments.
- No penalties or surprises.

Pros and Cons of Freelance and Firm Ownership

Pros

- Creative control.
- Higher earning potential.
- Flexible schedule.

Cons

- Income volatility.
- Administrative burdens.
- Must self-fund benefits.

Action Steps to Start Smart

1. **Pick a Business Structure**.
2. **Register and Set Up Financial Systems**.
3. **Plan for Taxes**.
4. **Invest in Insurance**.
5. **Develop Contracts and Proposals**.
6. **Build a Brand Presence**.

Architect-Specific Considerations

- **Professional liability** is non-negotiable.
- **Contracts** must be watertight to protect against scope creep and litigation.
- **Networking** remains crucial for referrals and repeat business.

The Project Management Mindset

Starting your firm is a phased project:

- **Programming**: Research and planning.
- **Schematic Design**: Choose entity and insurance.
- **Design Development**: Contracts and branding.
- **Construction Documents**: Systems and setup.
- **Construction Phase**: Launch and iterate.
- **Closeout**: Review financials and adjust quarterly.

Final Thoughts

The business side of architecture is just as important as the design side. A poorly structured or poorly run business can sink even the most talented designer.

Lay a solid foundation. Protect yourself legally and financially. Understand taxes. Embrace the role of architect and entrepreneur.

You are more capable than you think — and you're building a future you can be proud of.

Financial planning isn't about being perfect — it's about laying the groundwork and refining it over time.

The smartest architects don't just design beautiful buildings — they design sustainable lives.

Keep reviewing and updating your financial blueprint as your practice grows.

Let's continue building something lasting.

Chapter 15: Insurance Essentials

Introduction: Protection as a Cornerstone

Architecture is about designing structures that endure. In the same way, your financial life must be protected by solid support systems. Insurance isn't just a safety net; it's a strategic pillar in the architecture of financial security.

As an architect — especially one who is self-employed or owns a firm — understanding the right insurance policies is not optional. Health insurance, disability insurance, liability coverage, life insurance: these are not just checkboxes. They're part of safeguarding the career and financial life you're building.

Let's walk through how to structure your personal and professional insurance plan, with the same thoughtfulness you bring to a set of construction documents.

Health Insurance Options if Self-Employed

Why Health Insurance Matters

Architects know risk. Skipping health insurance is one risk you don't want to take. Without coverage, a single injury or illness could derail your finances for years.

Options for Self-Employed Architects

1. Health Insurance Marketplace (ACA Plans)

What It Is

- Federally or state-run marketplace for individual insurance.

Pros

- Guaranteed coverage.
- Subsidies available based on income.
- Wide range of plans.

Cons

- Can be expensive without subsidies.
- Limited to open enrollment periods unless qualifying event occurs.

2. Private Health Insurance

What It Is

- Purchase directly from insurers.

Pros

- Broader options.
- May find plans not listed on marketplaces.

Cons

- No income-based subsidies.
- May be costly.

3. Health Sharing Ministries

What It Is

- Faith-based organizations where members share healthcare costs.

Pros

- Lower monthly costs.

Cons

- Not traditional insurance.
- No legal guarantee of payment.

4. COBRA

What It Is

- Continuation of a former employer's health plan.

Pros

- Keeps existing coverage.

Cons

- High cost (you pay full premium + administrative fee).

5. Association Health Plans

What It Is

- Group health insurance through professional associations.

Pros

- Group rates.
- Often good for small firms.

Example

Some AIA chapters offer access to association health plans.

Key Terms to Know

- **Premium**: Monthly cost.
- **Deductible**: Amount you pay before insurance starts covering expenses.
- **Co-pay**: Set fee for office visits, prescriptions.
- **Out-of-pocket maximum**: The most you'll pay in a year.

Action Step

Compare total annual costs (premiums + expected out-of-pocket) across multiple plans.

Disability Insurance, Liability Insurance, and Life Insurance for Architects

Disability Insurance

Why It's Critical

Your ability to earn an income is your greatest asset. Disability insurance replaces a portion of your income if you can't work due to injury or illness.

Types

1. Short-Term Disability (STD)

- Covers a few months.
- Typically 60%-70% of salary.

2. Long-Term Disability (LTD)

- Kicks in after 3-6 months.
- Coverage until retirement age in some cases.

Key Features

- **Own-Occupation Coverage**: Pays benefits if you can't work in your specific occupation, even if you could work in another field.
- **Elimination Period**: Waiting period before benefits start.
- **Benefit Period**: How long payments last.

Action Step

Prioritize "own-occupation" policies. Review elimination and benefit periods.

Professional Liability Insurance

Also Called

- Errors and Omissions (E&O) Insurance.

Why You Need It

Even the best architects face risk:

- Design flaws.
- Missed deadlines.
- Cost overruns.

A single lawsuit could be financially devastating.

What It Covers

- Legal defense costs.
- Settlements and judgments.

Key Features

- **Claims-Made Coverage**: Only covers claims made while the policy is active.
- **Prior Acts Coverage**: Covers work done before the policy started.

Action Step

Ensure you have "prior acts" coverage if switching policies.

General Liability Insurance

What It Covers

- Bodily injury.
- Property damage.
- Advertising injury.

Why It Matters

If a client slips and falls during a site visit or if you're accused of slander in marketing materials, general liability protects you.

Life Insurance

Why It Matters

Life insurance protects your family or business partners if you die prematurely.

Types

1. Term Life Insurance

- Coverage for a set number of years.
- Inexpensive.

2. Permanent Life Insurance

- Lasts your lifetime.
- Includes an investment component.

How Much Coverage?

- 10-15 times your annual income.
- Enough to cover:
- Mortgage.
- Children's education.
- Daily living expenses.
- Business succession plans.

Action Step

Start with term insurance while building assets. Reassess needs every 5 years.

Real-World Scenario

Imagine:

- Solo architect.
- Income: $110,000/year.
- Health insurance premium: $600/month.
- Disability policy: $120/month.
- Professional liability: $2,000/year.
- Life insurance: $30/month (term policy).

Total insurance cost: ~$900/month.

A significant cost, but without it:

- A disability could wipe out income.
- A lawsuit could destroy your business.
- Premature death could leave dependents without support.

Pros and Cons of Comprehensive Insurance Planning

Pros

- Protects against major risks.
- Reduces financial stress.
- Safeguards family and business.

Cons

- Premium costs.
- Complexity of policy choices.

Common Mistakes to Avoid

- **Underestimating disability risk**.
- **Relying solely on savings**.
- **Ignoring "own-occupation" riders**.
- **Skipping professional liability coverage**.

Architect-Specific Considerations

- Architects often work beyond 65 — ensure disability benefits extend if you plan to.
- Claims on liability policies can occur years after project completion.
- If you partner with others, buy-sell agreements funded by life insurance can protect the business.

Strategies for Managing Costs

1. Shop Around

- Compare multiple providers.

2. Bundle Policies

- Some insurers offer discounts for bundling general liability and professional liability.

3. Health Savings Accounts (HSAs)

- If you have a high-deductible health plan, contribute to an HSA.
- Triple tax advantage: pre-tax contributions, tax-free growth, tax-free withdrawals for medical expenses.

The Project Management Mindset

Treat your insurance like a master plan:

- **Programming**: Assess your risks.
- **Schematic Design**: Explore insurance types.
- **Design Development**: Select and customize policies.
- **Construction Documents**: Formalize your protection plan.
- **Construction Phase**: Implement.
- **Closeout**: Review annually and adjust.

Final Thoughts

Insurance doesn't stop bad things from happening. It ensures that when they do, your financial house doesn't collapse.

The smartest architects don't just design beautiful buildings — they design sustainable lives.

Build your insurance plan thoughtfully, and review it as your career, family, and business grow.

You are more capable than you think — and you're building a future you can be proud of.

Financial planning isn't about being perfect — it's about laying the groundwork and refining it over time.

Let's continue building something lasting.

Chapter 16: Homeownership and Real Estate

Introduction: Architects, Homes, and Financial Reality

For architects, homeownership carries a special weight. You don't just see a house as a place to live — you see it as a structure, a system, a form, and a function. But that deep knowledge can be both an asset and a liability when navigating home buying or real estate investing.

Whether you're buying your first home, renovating a fixer-upper, or eyeing an investment property, the stakes are high. A real estate mistake can be costly, but done right, it can also be a powerful wealth-building tool.

This chapter will help you approach real estate decisions with the same rigor and planning you bring to your design work.

How Your Knowledge as an Architect Helps (and Sometimes Hurts)

The Advantages

1. Design Eye

- Ability to see potential where others see problems.
- Spotting quality construction versus poor workmanship.
- Understanding renovation scope and cost.

2. Planning and Project Management Skills

- Phased renovations.
- Managing budgets and timelines.
- Working with contractors.

3. Spatial Intelligence

- Assessing floorplans, flow, and adaptability.
- Visualizing improvements.

4. Professional Network

- Connections to contractors, engineers, inspectors.

The Disadvantages

1. Overconfidence

- Believing you can handle more than you realistically can.
- Underestimating time, cost, and disruption.

2. Perfectionism

- Holding out for the "ideal" house.
- Over-improving beyond neighborhood value.

3. Emotional Investment

- Seeing a house as a design project instead of a financial asset.

Action Step

Before buying or renovating, clarify your goals:

- Is this a home or a project?
- Is this about financial growth or design fulfillment?

Homeownership Basics: Buying Your First or Next Home

How Much Home Can You Afford?

Standard Rule:

- Housing costs (mortgage, taxes, insurance) ≤ 28%-30% of gross monthly income.
- Total debt payments (including housing) ≤ 36%-40%.

Consider:

- Student loans.
- Car loans.
- Credit cards.

Down Payments

Typical Range:

- 5%-20%.

20% avoids private mortgage insurance (PMI).

First-time homebuyer programs may allow as low as 3%.

Mortgages 101

- **Fixed-Rate Mortgage**: Same interest rate for the life of the loan.
- **Adjustable-Rate Mortgage (ARM)**: Lower initial rate, but can fluctuate.

Hidden Costs of Homeownership

- Property taxes.
- Homeowner's insurance.
- Maintenance and repairs.
- HOA fees.
- Utilities.

Action Step

Budget 1%-3% of home value annually for maintenance.

Renovating Your Home

Budget Realistically

- Renovations almost always cost more and take longer than expected.

Industry Rule of Thumb:

- Add 10%-20% contingency to any renovation budget.

DIY vs. Hiring Out

- **DIY**: Save money, but watch time and skill limitations.
- **Hiring Out**: Costly upfront but may save money long-term.

Permits and Regulations

- Skipping permits can hurt resale value and cause legal issues.

Action Step

Treat your renovation like a project:

- Clear scope.
- Realistic timeline.
- Contingency budget.

Investment Properties: Good Idea or Distraction?

Pros of Real Estate Investing

1. Cash Flow

- Rental income.

2. Appreciation

- Properties generally increase in value over time.

3. Tax Advantages

- Depreciation.
- Deductible expenses.

4. Leverage

- Borrowed money amplifies returns (but also risk).

Cons of Real Estate Investing

1. Management Headaches

- Tenant issues.
- Maintenance calls at 2 AM.

2. Capital Requirements

- Down payments.
- Repairs.
- Vacancy costs.

3. Market Risks

- Economic downturns.
- Property value declines.

4. Opportunity Cost

- Money tied up in real estate is not available for stocks, retirement funds, or business growth.

Architect-Specific Advantages

- Ability to assess property quality.
- Identify undervalued properties with potential.
- Manage renovations strategically.

Architect-Specific Risks

- Getting emotionally involved in "over-renovating."
- Overextending on multiple properties.

Key Metrics to Know

- **Cap Rate**: Net operating income / property value.
- **Cash-on-Cash Return**: Annual cash flow / cash invested.
- **Gross Rent Multiplier**: Property price / annual rent.

Should You Invest in Real Estate?

Ask Yourself:

- Can you afford the down payment and reserves without jeopardizing other goals?
- Do you have the time and energy to manage properties or vet property managers?
- Are you comfortable with the risks?

Action Step

Run the numbers on a prospective property. Don't assume "good design" will solve poor financials.

Real-World Scenario

Imagine:

- Architect earning $120,000/year.
- Buys a duplex for $400,000.
- Rents out one unit for $1,800/month.
- Lives in the other.

Result:

- Rental income covers most of the mortgage.
- Builds equity faster.

But:

- Must manage tenants.
- Absorb repair costs.
- Handle risk of vacancy.

Pros and Cons of Homeownership for Architects

Pros

- Forced savings via mortgage principal payments.
- Stability.
- Creative control over your living space.

Cons

- High upfront costs.
- Less flexibility to relocate.
- Ongoing maintenance and repair costs.

Common Mistakes Architects Make

- Over-renovating and not recouping costs.
- Prioritizing aesthetics over functionality.
- Underestimating project scope and costs.
- Failing to plan for liquidity needs.

The Project Management Mindset

Treat homeownership and real estate investing like professional projects:

- **Programming**: Define your goals (home vs. investment).
- **Schematic Design**: Identify target properties and budgets.
- **Design Development**: Run financial analyses.
- **Construction Documents**: Get pre-approvals, secure financing.
- **Construction Phase**: Purchase and manage renovations.
- **Closeout**: Evaluate ROI and lessons learned.

Final Thoughts

Real estate can be a powerful tool in your financial blueprint — if approached with the right balance of design passion and financial discipline.

As an architect, you have an edge — but only if you recognize when your strengths become blind spots.

Build wisely.

You are more capable than you think — and you're building a future you can be proud of.

Financial planning isn't about being perfect — it's about laying the groundwork and refining it over time.

The smartest architects don't just design beautiful buildings — they design sustainable lives.

Let's continue building something lasting.

Chapter 17: Studio Envy — Upgrading Your Life Thoughtfully

Introduction: The Quiet Pressure of Studio Culture

Architecture is a field where aesthetics, presentation, and style aren't just admired—they're expected. When you work in a studio surrounded by colleagues who drive sleek cars, wear minimalist designer outfits, and jet off on curated vacations, it's easy to fall into the trap of "studio envy."

Unlike many professions where income signals can be more muted, architecture has a cultural pressure to *look* the part.

But financial security isn't about appearances. It's about making deliberate choices—and that includes how you upgrade your lifestyle as your income grows.

This chapter will help you create a system for budgeting your raises and bonuses thoughtfully—so you can build a life that is truly elevated, not just aesthetically but financially.

The Studio Envy Trap

Why It's Dangerous

- Spending to match your peers can lead to lifestyle inflation.
- Raises get absorbed into bigger car payments, fancier apartments, and pricier vacations.
- Instead of building wealth, you build a treadmill.

What You're Really Seeing

- Appearances.
- Not debt levels, savings rates, or financial stress.

Action Step

Next time you're tempted to compare, remind yourself: "I'm building financial freedom, not financial appearances."

Budgeting Raises and Bonuses Wisely

Step 1: Celebrate — But Set a Limit

It's okay to enjoy a small splurge when you get a raise or bonus.
Rule of Thumb:

- Take 10%-20% of a bonus or first raise and spend it guilt-free.
- Allocate the rest to long-term goals.

Step 2: The 50/30/20 Framework (Revised for Architects)

Standard:

- 50% Needs (housing, utilities, groceries).
- 30% Wants (dining, travel, shopping).

- 20% Savings and debt payoff.

Revised for Architects:

- 45% Needs (including licensure, continuing ed, and professional development).
- 25% Wants.
- 30% Savings and debt payoff.

Why More to Savings?

- Architecture salaries often grow slowly.
- Early and aggressive savings gives you flexibility later.

Step 3: The Automatic Upgrade Rule

When you get a raise:

- Increase retirement contributions.
- Increase automatic savings transfers.

Automate the lifestyle upgrade to future you, not present you.

Step 4: The 1-Year Rule for Big Upgrades

Wait one year after a raise or bonus to:

- Move to a bigger apartment.
- Lease a fancier car.
- Take an extravagant vacation.

Why?

- It gives you a cooling-off period.
- Ensures the raise is stable and not a one-off.

Common Financial Pitfalls for Architects

- Leasing expensive cars too soon.
- Overextending on rent or mortgages.
- Putting professional image over personal solvency.

Action Step

List three financial goals you'd rather hit than leasing a $700/month car.

- Max out your 401(k).
- Pay off student loans faster.
- Build a 6-month emergency fund.

Investing Bonuses Wisely

If You Get a Bonus

Before you spend it:

1. Set aside 30% for taxes (if not automatically withheld).
2. Allocate 50%-70% toward long-term goals.
3. Use a small portion (10%-20%) for discretionary fun.

Long-Term Goals to Fund

- 401(k) or IRA contributions.
- Home down payment savings.
- Emergency fund top-off.
- Continuing education courses or certifications.

- Business startup fund (if you want to open your own firm).

The Psychology of Upgrading

Why We Feel Pressure

- Mirror neurons: We subconsciously imitate peer behavior.
- Social validation: Fancy upgrades feel like proof of "making it."

How to Resist

- Reframe: "I'm designing a beautiful life, not just a beautiful image."
- Anchor: Regularly revisit your true goals (financial independence, business ownership, etc.).

Real-World Scenario

Imagine:

- Architect earns $80,000.
- Gets a $10,000 raise.

Option A: Upgrade to luxury apartment, nicer car.

- Extra $800/month gone.
- No real wealth growth.

Option B: Increase 401(k) contribution by 5%.

- Open Roth IRA.
- Take $1,000 and book a weekend getaway.
- Rest goes into high-yield savings.

Result:

- Financial cushion grows.
- Future flexibility secured.
- Still enjoy a treat.

Lifestyle Design for Architects

Elements of a Well-Designed Financial Life

- Functional: Covers all needs comfortably.
- Sustainable: Can weather economic downturns.
- Beautiful: Has room for small luxuries that bring true joy.

Just like good architecture, good financial design balances:

- Form (how your life looks).
- Function (how your finances work).

Action Step

Design a "Minimum Viable Lifestyle":

- Comfortable but modest.
- Allows for max savings.

Design a "Dream Lifestyle":

- What you want long-term.
- Create a savings and career plan to get there.

The Project Management Mindset

Treat your financial life upgrades like project phases:

- **Programming**: Identify true goals.
- **Schematic Design**: Plan your raise allocation.
- **Design Development**: Automate savings.
- **Construction Documents**: Set clear budgets.
- **Construction Phase**: Implement upgrades slowly.
- **Closeout**: Review and refine annually.

Final Thoughts

Financial freedom doesn't come from chasing appearances. It comes from designing a life that's balanced, resilient, and aligned with your deepest values.

Upgrading thoughtfully means you can enjoy today without sacrificing tomorrow.

You are more capable than you think — and you're building a future you can be proud of.

Financial planning isn't about being perfect — it's about laying the groundwork and refining it over time.

The smartest architects don't just design beautiful buildings — they design sustainable lives.

Let's continue building something lasting.

Chapter 18: Investing Beyond Retirement Accounts

Introduction: Beyond the 401(k)

Retirement accounts are essential, but they are just the beginning. Many architects hit a point where maxing out a 401(k) or IRA is not enough to meet their bigger financial goals—buying a dream home, starting a firm, retiring early, or funding large creative projects.

Diversifying your financial blueprint requires thinking beyond tax-advantaged accounts.

This chapter explores brokerage accounts, real estate, REITs, and alternative investments to help you design a financial portfolio as durable and thoughtful as any structure you've ever drawn.

Brokerage Accounts: The Next Step

What Is a Brokerage Account?

- A taxable investment account.
- No contribution limits.
- No early withdrawal penalties.
- Wide investment choices: stocks, bonds, ETFs, mutual funds.

Tax Implications

- Capital gains taxes on profits.
- Dividends taxed annually.

Long-Term Gains (held > 1 year):

- 0%, 15%, or 20%, depending on income.

Short-Term Gains (held ≤ 1 year):

- Taxed as ordinary income.

Why Architects Should Care

- Flexibility for mid-term goals (buying land, funding a project).
- Opportunity to invest more aggressively if retirement accounts are maxed out.

How to Use Brokerage Accounts

- Supplement retirement savings.
- Build a "freedom fund" for career transitions.
- Fund a future home purchase.

Real-World Scenario

Imagine:

- Architect maxes out 401(k) and IRA.
- Opens brokerage account.
- Invests $1,000/month.

Result over 20 years (assuming 7% return):

- Over $500,000.
- Flexible, accessible wealth.

Action Step

Open a low-cost brokerage account and set up automatic monthly contributions.

Real Estate: Owning More Than Your Home

Why Real Estate Appeals to Architects

- Tangibility: Real property.
- Skill overlap: Design, project management.
- Potential for passive income.

Types of Real Estate Investments

1. Direct Ownership

- Residential rental properties.
- Commercial buildings.
- Land development.

2. Real Estate Investment Trusts (REITs)

- Companies that own, operate, or finance real estate.
- Traded like stocks.

3. Real Estate Crowdfunding

- Pool money with other investors.
- Lower entry costs.

Pros of Direct Real Estate Investment

- Potential cash flow.
- Appreciation.
- Tax advantages (depreciation, 1031 exchanges).

Cons

- Management headaches.
- Illiquidity.
- High capital needs.

REITs: Real Estate Without the Headaches

Pros

- Easy to buy and sell.
- Dividend income.
- Diversification.

Cons

- Sensitive to interest rates.
- Market volatility.

Alternative Investments

What Are They?

- Investments outside traditional stocks and bonds.

Examples:

- Private equity.
- Venture capital.
- Hedge funds.
- Art and collectibles.
- Cryptocurrency.

Pros

- Diversification.
- Potential for high returns.

Cons

- Illiquidity.
- High fees.
- High risk.

Should Architects Use Alternative Investments?

Only after:

- Maxing out retirement accounts.
- Building an emergency fund.
- Establishing stable brokerage and real estate investments.

Diversifying Your Financial Blueprint

Why Diversification Matters

Just as good architecture balances form and function, good financial planning balances risk and reward.

Diversification helps:

- Smooth returns.
- Reduce risk.
- Protect against sector downturns.

Example Diversified Portfolio

- 60% Stocks (U.S. and International).
- 20% Bonds.
- 10% Real Estate (REITs or direct).
- 5% Alternatives.
- 5% Cash.

Real-World Scenario

Imagine:

- 35-year-old architect.
- $150,000/year income.
- Maxed out 401(k) and Roth IRA.
- $50,000 brokerage account.
- Owns duplex rental property.

Net worth growing via:

- Tax-advantaged retirement savings.

- Taxable brokerage flexibility.
- Real estate cash flow and appreciation.

Action Steps to Diversify

1. Maximize 401(k) and IRA contributions.
2. Open a brokerage account.
3. Explore real estate (direct or REITs).
4. Consider alternative investments carefully.
5. Rebalance portfolio annually.

Common Mistakes to Avoid

- Chasing high returns with too much risk.
- Ignoring fees (especially in alternative investments).
- Over-concentrating in real estate.
- Neglecting tax implications.

The Project Management Mindset

Apply architectural project thinking:

- **Programming**: Define investment goals.
- **Schematic Design**: Draft a rough asset allocation.
- **Design Development**: Choose investment vehicles.
- **Construction Documents**: Formalize accounts and automatic contributions.
- **Construction Phase**: Start investing.
- **Closeout**: Review and rebalance.

Final Thoughts

Investing beyond retirement accounts is about building a durable, flexible financial structure.

Architects are uniquely suited to this work — we understand systems, plans, and patience.

You are more capable than you think — and you're building a future you can be proud of.

Financial planning isn't about being perfect — it's about laying the groundwork and refining it over time.

The smartest architects don't just design beautiful buildings — they design sustainable lives.

Let's continue building something lasting.

Chapter 19: Saving for Family Goals

Introduction: Designing for Generations

As architects, we often think in terms of legacy. A well-designed building outlives its creator, serving communities for generations.

The same can be said for financial planning. It's not just about you — it's about the people you love.

Whether it's saving for your kids' education, preparing for their future, or ensuring your parents are cared for, thoughtful financial design today creates stability tomorrow.

In this chapter, we'll explore strategies for saving toward family goals, balancing today's demands with tomorrow's promises.

Kids and College Savings

Why College Planning Matters

- College costs have risen dramatically.
- Student loan debt can impact your child's financial future.

Early planning helps:

- Reduce debt burden.

- Open choices (in-state, out-of-state, private).
- Create a platform for generational advancement.

529 Plans: The Architect's Blueprint for Education Savings

What Is a 529 Plan?

- Tax-advantaged savings plan.
- Funds can be used for qualified education expenses.

Key Features

- Tax-free growth.
- Withdrawals for qualified expenses are tax-free.
- High contribution limits.
- Some states offer tax deductions or credits.

529 Plan vs. Other Savings Vehicles

Feature	529 Plan	Roth IRA	Savings Account
Tax-Free Growth	Yes	Yes (if used for retirement)	No
Penalties	Only if used for non-education	Early withdrawal penalties	None
Financial Aid Impact	Moderate	Moderate	High

How Much to Save

Rule of Thumb:

- Aim to cover 50% of the projected cost.
- Encourage kids to contribute via work, scholarships.

Tools:

- Use online calculators.
- Project cost for in-state vs. private schools.

Action Step

Open a 529 plan as soon as possible. Set up automatic monthly contributions—even $50/month compounds over time.

Caring for Aging Parents

The Financial Reality

- Longer life expectancies.
- Rising healthcare costs.
- Potential need for long-term care.

Many architects will face the "sandwich generation" dilemma—supporting kids and aging parents simultaneously.

Key Considerations

- Discuss finances openly with parents.
- Understand their resources (pensions, Social Security, savings).
- Plan for long-term care insurance if needed.

Action Steps for Supporting Parents

1. Understand Their Situation

- Do they have a will, health directive, power of attorney?
- What are their income sources?

2. Plan for Emergencies

- Build a separate "parent care fund."
- Consider long-term care insurance early—before health issues arise.

3. Balance Your Goals

- Don't jeopardize your own retirement.
- Financially helping parents should not derail your future.

Common Financial Pitfalls

- Draining your retirement savings to pay for their care.
- Ignoring your spouse's or children's financial needs.
- Failing to set clear boundaries.

Using Architect Skills to Plan Family Finances

Systems Thinking

Approach family finances like a master plan:

- Short-term needs: Day-to-day expenses.
- Mid-term needs: College tuition.
- Long-term needs: Retirement, healthcare.

Create a timeline and budget accordingly.

Design for Flexibility

Life changes. Financial plans should, too.

- Review family financial goals annually.
- Adjust 529 contributions if income changes.
- Update care plans for parents as health evolves.

Real-World Scenario

Imagine:

- 40-year-old architect.
- 2 kids, ages 6 and 9.
- Parents aged 68 and 70.

Financial Moves:

- Open 529 plans.
- Increase retirement contributions.
- Start a separate savings account for parent emergencies.
- Purchase long-term care insurance for parents if they don't have it.

Prioritizing Goals

In order of importance:

1. Fund your retirement first.
2. Build emergency savings.
3. Save for college.
4. Prepare for parental care.

Why Retirement Comes First

- No scholarships or loans for retirement.
- Protects your kids from supporting you later.

Tax-Advantaged Options

- 529 Plan.
- Health Savings Accounts (HSAs).
- 401(k)s and IRAs.

Using Bonuses and Windfalls Wisely

- Allocate portions to:
- Kids' college fund.
- Parents' emergency fund.
- Your retirement.

Avoid the temptation to spend it all.

Protecting Your Family With Insurance

- Life insurance: Ensure dependents are cared for.
- Disability insurance: Protect your earning power.
- Long-term care insurance for parents.

Action Plan

1. Review your current financial picture.
2. Prioritize retirement savings.
3. Open or fund 529 plans.
4. Discuss finances with parents.
5. Establish emergency savings for parental care.

6. Reassess annually.

The Project Management Mindset

Apply architectural project management to family goals:

- **Programming**: Identify all family financial needs.
- **Schematic Design**: Draft a plan to fund each goal.
- **Design Development**: Set up appropriate savings vehicles.
- **Construction Documents**: Formalize contribution schedules.
- **Construction Phase**: Execute.
- **Closeout**: Review and adjust annually.

Final Thoughts

Saving for family goals is an act of love and legacy.

It's about ensuring your kids have options.

It's about giving your parents dignity.

It's about balancing today's sacrifices with tomorrow's dreams.

You are more capable than you think — and you're building a future you can be proud of.

Financial planning isn't about being perfect — it's about laying the groundwork and refining it over time.

The smartest architects don't just design beautiful buildings — they design sustainable lives.

Let's continue building something lasting.

Chapter 20: Understanding the Value of Your Professional Network

Introduction: Networking as Structural Integrity

In architecture, the strength of a structure depends on carefully engineered connections. Your financial life is no different.

Your professional network—the relationships you cultivate with colleagues, mentors, clients, and collaborators—can have a profound, compounding impact on your career and wealth-building efforts. Networking isn't just about job leads or social handshakes; it's about building social capital, an asset that can quietly pay dividends over the span of your professional life.

In this chapter, we'll explore how to think strategically about networking as an architect, how social capital translates to financial capital, and how to build and maintain a network that strengthens your financial blueprint.

The Hidden Financial Benefits of Networking

What Is Social Capital?

Social capital is the currency of relationships. It's the reservoir of trust, goodwill, and mutual support you build with others over time.

Just as financial capital grows through smart investment, social capital grows through consistent, intentional relationship-building.

Financial Outcomes from Social Capital

Higher Earning Potential

- Access to opportunities not advertised publicly.
- Leverage in salary negotiations by understanding market rates.
- Peer endorsements can lead to accelerated career advancement.

Business Development

- Steady referrals from trusted colleagues and clients.
- Strategic collaborations.
- Access to high-value projects and RFPs.

Market Intelligence

- First-hand insights into market shifts.
- Knowledge of new developments, technologies, and business trends.

Career Resilience

- Access to new job leads during economic downturns.
- Insights on when it's time to move firms or adjust career focus.

Real-World Financial Impact

An architect with a strong professional network will:

- Land higher-paying jobs faster.
- Pay less for marketing their services.
- Face fewer gaps in employment.

- Find clients and projects with greater ease.

Networking, when done well, is a strategic investment in career stability and financial growth.

Building Social Capital That Pays Off Later

Step 1: Build Before You Need It

Networking is not something you start when you're in a bind. Build it slowly, consistently, before you need it.

- Attend industry conferences.
- Join professional organizations (like AIA).
- Stay in touch with alumni networks.

Long-term thinking wins.

Step 2: Give Before You Get

Genuine networking is about giving first.

- Share opportunities with others.
- Connect peers to resources or introductions.
- Celebrate others' successes.

Generosity creates a foundation of trust and reciprocity.

Step 3: Stay Top of Mind

Visibility is key.

- Periodically check in.

- Send a congratulatory note when someone earns a promotion.
- Comment on their professional updates.

Subtle, thoughtful gestures make you memorable.

Step 4: Diversify Your Network

Avoid the echo chamber.

- Connect with engineers, contractors, and real estate developers.
- Forge relationships with clients across industries.
- Network with professionals from finance, law, and tech.

Diverse networks are more resilient and create unexpected opportunities.

Compounding Returns of Networking

Like compound interest, the value of your network grows over time.

- A connection made today could lead to a major opportunity a decade later.
- Small gestures now can result in big favors later.

The best time to plant a tree was 20 years ago. The second-best time is today.

Strategic Networking for Architects

Targeted Networking

Focus your efforts on connections that align with your career goals.

- Senior architects who can mentor you.

- Project managers at firms where you'd like to work.
- Real estate developers for potential client relationships.

Be intentional.

Maintaining Long-Term Relationships

Architectural careers are marathons.

- Stay connected to former colleagues.
- Remember milestones: promotions, firm anniversaries.
- Be consistent, not transactional.

Common Networking Pitfalls

- Reaching out only when you need something.
- Focusing only on peers and neglecting other industry players.
- Neglecting to follow up after a great conversation.

Sincerity and consistency are key.

Action Steps

1. List 20 professional contacts you haven't spoken to in the last year.
2. Send personalized check-in messages to five of them.
3. Schedule one networking meeting per month.
4. Join at least one new professional organization.
5. Look for one opportunity to help someone else without expecting anything in return.

Real-World Scenarios

Scenario 1: The Power of Mentorship

A young architect regularly checks in with a senior architect she met during her internship. Years later, that mentor connects her to a dream job.

Scenario 2: The Ripple Effect of Referrals

An architect shares a job posting with a colleague who lands the role. The colleague later refers a lucrative client to the architect.

Networking generosity comes full circle.

Networking as a Financial Strategy

Zoning Your Network

- Allocate time weekly for relationship building.
- Design a system: CRM tools, reminders, and social media.

Infrastructure: Communication

- Professional email.
- LinkedIn updates.
- Handwritten notes for major milestones.

Community Building

- Host dinners.
- Organize small professional meetups.
- Speak at local design events.

Sustainability

- Refresh connections regularly.
- Reconnect when people change jobs or cities.

Leveraging Your Network for Business Growth

If you're running your own practice, your network becomes your marketing machine.

- Referrals reduce customer acquisition costs.
- Warm leads close faster and at higher rates.
- Reputational equity builds without expensive advertising.

Metrics to Track

- Number of outreach emails sent.
- Number of meetings or coffee catch-ups.
- Number of referrals made.

Networking is a long game. Progress is cumulative.

Digital Networking

LinkedIn Best Practices

- Keep your profile updated.
- Share insights and project wins.
- Comment thoughtfully on others' posts.

Online Communities

- Join architecture-focused forums.
- Engage in local design groups on LinkedIn or Facebook.
- Attend virtual industry events.

Digital platforms amplify your network when used strategically.

Final Thoughts

Your network is one of the most valuable, underrated financial assets you have as an architect.

It influences job security, income potential, business development, and career resilience.

You are more capable than you think — and you're building a future you can be proud of.

Financial planning isn't about being perfect — it's about laying the groundwork and refining it over time.

The smartest architects don't just design beautiful buildings — they design sustainable lives.

Build your network. Protect it. Nurture it.

Let's keep building something lasting.

Part IV: Architecting Your Legacy — Late Career and Retirement Planning

After years of designing structures for others, it's time to turn that precision and foresight inward — to design the legacy you leave behind. Part IV helps seasoned architects transition from active earning to thoughtful preservation, applying the same strategic mindset used in architecture to their financial future.

This section covers the financial nuances of late career moves, succession planning for those leading firms, and strategies to ensure that your wealth endures beyond your working years. We explore optimizing retirement account withdrawals, designing an estate plan that reflects both personal and professional legacies, and how to thoughtfully mentor the next generation. Whether you're contemplating stepping back, selling a practice, or focusing on philanthropy and family, this part is your guide to a well-constructed exit and an enduring impact.

Just as every great building stands as a testament to careful planning and execution, your financial legacy can stand strong for your loved ones and your profession. Here, we shift the focus from career building to wealth preserving — ensuring you transition not just out of a job, but into a life of purpose, security, and significance.

Chapter 21: Senior Roles and Equity Opportunities

Becoming a senior leader in an architecture firm isn't just about prestige; it's about leveraging decades of skill into ownership and wealth-building opportunities. For many architects, reaching partner status or securing equity in a firm represents the financial pinnacle of a long career. But the path to partnership and profit-sharing isn't always straightforward.

In this chapter, we'll examine the financial dimensions of senior leadership roles, partner tracks, and equity opportunities in architecture firms—and how to evaluate if the rewards align with the risks.

The Architecture of Senior Roles

As you advance in your career, the day-to-day technical work of architecture often shifts toward business development, client management, and strategic leadership. Senior roles include titles like:

- Principal Architect
- Partner
- Design Director
- Managing Director
- Studio Leader

With these roles come new responsibilities: driving revenue, managing firm reputation, recruiting talent, and overseeing projects at the firmwide level.

Financial Rewards of Senior Positions

Salaries for senior architects vary based on firm size, geography, and firm profitability, but typically these positions can command:

- Six-figure salaries ($120,000–$250,000+)
- Annual bonuses based on firm performance
- Profit-sharing allocations
- Equity stakes with dividends

However, it's crucial to understand the fine print.

Profit-Sharing Models Explained

Profit-sharing is one way firms align leadership incentives. Generally, a portion of the firm's profits (often after expenses and salaries) is distributed among partners.

There are different profit-sharing structures:

- **Equal share:** All partners receive an equal cut.
- **Performance-based share:** Profits are distributed based on personal or firmwide performance metrics.
- **Ownership percentage share:** Dividends are based on equity ownership percentages.

Equity Ownership: What It Really Means

Owning equity in a firm means you hold an ownership stake, and with that come both rights and responsibilities. Equity may come in different forms:

- **Voting Rights:** Decisions about firm direction, hiring, or selling the firm.
- **Dividend Rights:** A share of profits.
- **Obligations:** In some firms, equity partners may be required to "buy in," committing capital to the firm.

Equity also brings risks:

- Financial liability if the firm underperforms.
- Potential capital calls to shore up the business.
- Losses in the case of firm dissolution.

Buy-In Requirements

Many firms require incoming partners to "buy in"—pay a set amount for their ownership stake. This can range from $50,000 to $500,000+, depending on the firm's valuation.

Buy-ins can be structured:

- **Lump sum payment.**
- **Financing through the firm (payroll deductions over time).**
- **Bank financing (less common, but possible).

Evaluating an Offer to Join the Partnership

When presented with a partner-track or equity opportunity, consider:

- **Firm's financial health.** Review financial statements.
- **Client concentration.** Is the firm's revenue dependent on a few clients?
- **Leadership dynamics.** Will you have real influence?
- **Exit strategy.** How do partners cash out when they leave?

Stock Options and Alternative Equity Structures

Some firms may not offer traditional partnership equity but may offer:

- **Phantom Stock:** Synthetic equity that pays out bonuses tied to firm valuation.
- **Stock Appreciation Rights (SARs):** Rights to profit from firm growth.
- **Employee Stock Ownership Plans (ESOPs):** Rare in architecture,

but possible.

Each has pros and cons. Phantom stock offers upside without requiring a capital commitment, but it's not true ownership.

Tax Implications

Equity ownership can have significant tax implications:

- **Pass-through income:** Many architecture firms are structured as partnerships or LLCs, meaning profits pass through to partners' personal tax returns.
- **Self-employment taxes:** As an owner, you'll be responsible for full self-employment tax on your share.
- **Capital gains:** If you eventually sell your stake, you may owe capital gains taxes.

Case Study: Moving from Salary to Equity

Let's consider "Michael," a mid-career architect offered partnership at a 40-person firm. His salary would stay the same ($160,000), but he would need to buy in for $125,000.

- **Annual profit share:** Historically around $40,000/year.
- **Firm health:** Steady, diversified client base.
- **Exit policy:** Buyout at book value.

Michael must weigh:

- The opportunity cost of $125,000 invested elsewhere.
- The stability of the firm's profits.
- His personal risk tolerance.

Pros and Cons of Becoming a Partner

Pros:

- Significant wealth-building potential.
- More influence over firm direction.
- Professional prestige.
- Alignment of interests with other partners.

Cons:

- Capital at risk.
- Responsibility for firm financial performance.
- Time demands often increase.
- Complex tax filings and financial planning needs.

Negotiating Partnership Terms

When approaching partnership, negotiation is key. Clarify:

- Buy-in amount and structure.
- Expected distributions.
- Financial transparency.
- Exit terms.
- Expectations for business development.

Alternatives to Full Equity Partnership

If full partnership isn't the right fit, explore:

- **Profit-sharing without equity.**
- **Bonus structures tied to firm performance.**
- **Leadership roles with higher base salaries but no ownership.

The Soft Skills That Matter

Beyond technical ability, succeeding as a senior leader requires:

- Business development acumen.
- Leadership and team management skills.

- Financial literacy.
- Negotiation abilities.

Building a Long-Term Strategy

If partnership is your goal:

- Seek mentors within your firm.
- Volunteer for leadership roles.
- Get comfortable with financial statements.
- Understand the business of architecture.

Exit Planning: Getting Out Without Losing Out

Eventually, you may want to retire or move on. Understanding your firm's exit policies is crucial:

- **Buy-sell agreements:** How the firm values your share.
- **Payout timelines:** Lump sum vs. installments.
- **Successor planning:** Is there a junior partner ready to buy you out?

Action Steps

- **Benchmark your salary and benefits.** Know what's standard for your level and geography.
- **Understand your firm's ownership structures.**
- **Ask for financial transparency before buying in.**
- **Model your financial future with and without partnership.

Final Thoughts

Moving into a senior role or ownership stake in an architecture firm can be one of the most financially rewarding steps of your career—if you approach it with the same thoroughness and precision you bring to your design work. It's not just about the title or the corner office. It's about aligning your professional skills, your financial goals, and your personal risk tolerance.

In architecture, as in finance, structure matters. Take the time to understand the scaffolding behind senior leadership and ownership opportunities. Build not just your career, but your financial future, with intention and clarity.

You are more capable than you think — and you're building a legacy you can be proud of.

Keep reviewing, refining, and revisiting your blueprint for career and financial success—just like you'd revisit a master plan to ensure its integrity over decades.

Your future, like your best designs, deserves nothing less.

Chapter 22: Advanced Retirement Planning

In the design and execution of a successful architectural career, one thing is as important as a structurally sound building: a financially sound retirement plan. As architects approach the late stages of their careers, the financial moves they make today have profound impacts on the life they will live tomorrow. Advanced retirement planning is not just about "catching up." It's about finishing strong, leveraging every available tool to ensure your "retirement blueprint" is as carefully drawn and robust as your best projects.

The Unique Retirement Challenges of Architects

Architects face a number of unique challenges when it comes to retirement planning:

- **Delayed Peak Earnings**: Many architects don't reach their highest earning potential until mid or late career.
- **Long Hours and Stress**: The career's demands can delay focus on financial planning.
- **Variable Income**: Especially for firm owners or independent contractors.
- **Passion for the Work**: Architects often work later into life because they love what they do, not necessarily because they are financially

secure.

Given these factors, late-career architects must be deliberate, strategic, and proactive in optimizing their retirement savings.

Understanding Catch-Up Contributions

One of the most powerful tools available to late-career savers is the "catch-up" contribution.

What Are Catch-Up Contributions?

For individuals aged 50 and older, the IRS allows additional contributions beyond the regular limits to 401(k) plans and IRAs:

- **401(k), 403(b), and 457 Plans**: Regular limit ($22,500 for 2024) + catch-up limit ($7,500 for 2024).
- **Traditional and Roth IRAs**: Regular limit ($6,500 for 2024) + catch-up limit ($1,000).

This means you can contribute more and supercharge your retirement savings in the final decade or so of your career.

Why It Matters for Architects

Think of it as designing an addition to an existing structure. Catch-up contributions allow you to add substantial financial "square footage" to your retirement portfolio, compensating for years when saving was more challenging.

Key action step: Set a reminder at your 50th birthday to review your contribution rates and maximize these enhanced limits.

Tax Optimization for Late-Career Savers

Smart retirement planning is not just about saving money; it's about saving money **strategically**.

Understand Your Current Tax Bracket

Most architects in their peak earning years are in higher tax brackets. Strategies to lower taxable income now include:

- Maxing out pre-tax contributions to 401(k) or traditional IRA.
- Utilizing an HSA (Health Savings Account) if eligible.

Example: Pre-tax contributions reduce your taxable income, possibly moving you into a lower bracket and reducing your current tax bill.

Roth Conversions

As you move toward retirement, consider strategic **Roth conversions** during lower-income years or after retirement but before Required Minimum Distributions (RMDs) kick in.

What is it?

Moving funds from a pre-tax account (like a 401(k) or Traditional IRA) into a Roth IRA. You pay taxes now but enjoy tax-free growth and withdrawals later.

Why does it matter for architects?

Your goal is to "diversify" your tax exposure in retirement. Having both pre-tax and Roth accounts gives you flexibility to manage income (and taxes) when you're drawing down.

Capital Gains and Investment Income Planning

If you've built brokerage accounts (non-retirement accounts), late career is the time to:

- Harvest gains and losses strategically.
- Hold investments long enough to qualify for long-term capital gains rates.
- Consider tax-efficient investments like index funds or municipal bonds.

Aligning Investment Strategy with Timeline

Late career is the time to "de-risk" your portfolio, but not to eliminate growth entirely.

Glide Path Strategy

Think of your portfolio as a designed structure: you wouldn't pour a foundation with no reinforcement. Similarly, even late in your career, you need growth assets (equities) to hedge against inflation and longevity.

Typical glide path for late-career architects:

- 60% stocks / 40% bonds at age 50.
- Gradually moving toward 40% stocks / 60% bonds by early retirement.

Protecting Principal

You can create "buckets" for different time frames:

- **Short-term**: 1-3 years of expenses in cash or short-term bonds.
- **Mid-term**: 5-10 years in moderate investments.
- **Long-term**: 10+ years in growth-oriented investments.

This structure provides liquidity for early retirement years while allowing long-term growth.

Managing Debt and Risk

Entering retirement debt-free is ideal, but not always realistic.

Key Principles:

- **Pay off high-interest debt first** (credit cards, personal loans).
- **Consider paying down or refinancing mortgage** if rates are high.
- **Avoid new large debts** late in your career.

Insurance Review

- **Life insurance**: Do you still need it? Often not once kids are independent.
- **Disability insurance**: Less critical close to retirement.
- **Long-Term Care insurance**: Worth considering.

Social Security and Pension Decisions

Timing matters:

- **Full Retirement Age (FRA)** is typically 66-67.
- Delaying benefits until 70 maximizes your monthly payout.

Architects often delay retirement, but that doesn't mean you should delay planning.

Pension Considerations

If you are one of the lucky few with a pension, understand:

- **Single life vs. joint and survivor benefits**.

- **Lump sum payout vs. annuity**.

Each option has different tax and longevity implications.

Estate Planning and Legacy Design

This is your final "project," and like any good design, it requires:

- **A will**
- **A trust** (if appropriate)
- **Healthcare directives**
- **Powers of attorney**

Architects often think about the "legacy" they leave through buildings. Why not extend that thinking to your financial legacy?

Update your beneficiaries regularly, especially after major life events.

Real-World Case Study

Meet Lisa, 58

Lisa has been a project architect for 30 years, earns $140,000 annually, and recently became eligible for catch-up contributions. Her goals:

- Retire at 65.
- Travel extensively.
- Leave a legacy to her children.

Her Actions:

- Maxed out 401(k) contributions including catch-up.
- Increased Roth IRA contributions.
- Began Roth conversions during a sabbatical year with lower income.
- Shifted portfolio from 80/20 to 60/40 asset allocation.

- Met with a financial planner to set up a trust.

Result: She's on track to replace 85% of her income in retirement and has a diversified tax strategy.

Building a Late-Career "Punch List"

1. **Max out catch-up contributions.**
2. **Consider Roth conversions.**
3. **De-risk your portfolio gradually.**
4. **Eliminate or minimize debt.**
5. **Plan Social Security and pension strategies.**
6. **Update estate planning documents.**
7. **Maintain sufficient insurance coverage.**
8. **Review and update beneficiaries.**
9. **Consider charitable giving strategies for tax benefits.**
10. **Schedule annual financial "blueprint" reviews.**

Final Thoughts

Advanced retirement planning is not about racing to the finish. It's about pacing yourself and designing a structure that will stand the test of time.

You are more capable than you think. You've spent a lifetime solving complex problems for clients — now you're solving for your future.

The smartest architects don't just design beautiful buildings. They design sustainable, rewarding lives. And they do it one deliberate choice at a time.

Next Step

Review your current retirement plan today. Make adjustments like you would to a project master plan. Because just like architecture, great financial outcomes don't happen by accident. They happen by design.

Chapter 23: Estate Planning Basics for Architects

Why Estate Planning Matters for Architects

When you hear "estate planning," you might think it's only for the ultra-wealthy. But every architect — whether you're a principal running a thriving firm, a project manager nearing retirement, or a solo practitioner just launching your business — needs a plan for what happens to your assets, your firm, and your legacy. Estate planning is not just about money; it's about design. It's about intention. It's about protecting what you've built with the same thoughtfulness you'd bring to a project's master plan.

Wills: The Foundation of Your Financial Blueprint

At its core, a will is a set of instructions — much like an architectural program. It spells out your wishes for your property, appoints guardians for minor children, and names the executor who will carry out your wishes. Without a will, the state decides how to distribute your assets based on generic formulas. You lose control — and for an architect, that's not acceptable.

Key Points About Wills:

- **Simple Wills** cover the basics: who inherits what, who oversees the process.
- **Testamentary Trust Wills** create a trust within your will for minor children or other dependents.
- **Pour-Over Wills** work alongside a living trust to "catch" any assets not properly titled in the trust.

Drafting a will can cost a few hundred to a few thousand dollars depending on complexity — a small investment for clarity and control.

Trusts: Advanced Blueprinting for Your Assets

Think of a trust as a structure you design during your lifetime. It holds assets, manages them, and distributes them according to your detailed specifications.

Types of Trusts Architects Should Know:

- **Revocable Living Trust:** Allows you to maintain control during your lifetime. Avoids probate.
- **Irrevocable Trust:** Offers stronger asset protection and estate tax advantages, but you relinquish control.
- **Special Needs Trust:** Ensures that a dependent with special needs can inherit without losing government benefits.

Setting up a trust can cost more upfront — perhaps $1,000 to $5,000 — but it can save your estate many times that amount by avoiding probate fees, reducing estate taxes, and keeping your affairs private.

Power of Attorney: Protecting Your Decision-Making Ability

A power of attorney (POA) is a simple but powerful document. It allows someone you trust to make financial decisions on your behalf if you're incapacitated.

Why It's Important:

- Without a POA, your family may have to petition a court to manage your affairs.
- It's like having an emergency backup architect on a project — critical when timelines are tight and decisions must be made.

There are two main types:

- **Durable POA:** Stays in effect even if you become incapacitated.
- **Springing POA:** "Springs" into effect only if you become incapacitated.

Health Care Directives: Designing Your Medical Wishes

Just as important as financial decisions are health care directives. These include:

- **Living Will:** Specifies the types of medical treatments you want or don't want.
- **Health Care Power of Attorney:** Appoints someone to make medical decisions if you're unable.

Together, these documents ensure that your personal values — just like your design values — are honored when you can't speak for yourself.

Passing on Your Practice: Succession Planning

If you own your firm, your practice is part of your estate. It's a living entity, and without a plan, it can collapse under the weight of uncertainty.

Options for Succession:

- **Sell to Partners:** A buy-sell agreement ensures a smooth transition.
- **Groom an Internal Successor:** Identify and mentor a successor well

in advance.

- **Sell to an Outside Buyer:** Requires a valuation and a well-structured sale process.
- **Wind Down the Firm:** If no succession is feasible, plan a phased closure to protect clients and employees.

Key Documents:

- **Buy-Sell Agreements:** Pre-set the terms under which shares can be sold.
- **Operating Agreements:** Spell out what happens to the business if an owner dies.

Real-World Scenario: Case Studies

Case Study 1: Sarah, Solo Practitioner

Sarah is a 58-year-old architect running a solo practice. She has a daughter in college and a modest estate. Sarah creates:

- A revocable living trust to manage her firm and personal assets.
- A will naming her daughter as primary beneficiary.
- A durable power of attorney naming her business manager.
- A living will outlining her health care wishes.

By planning early, Sarah ensures her practice can be sold and her daughter's education funded without legal headaches.

Case Study 2: David and Michelle, Firm Partners

David and Michelle co-own a mid-sized firm. They:

- Draft buy-sell agreements with life insurance to fund a partner buyout.
- Create trusts to minimize estate taxes.
- Establish clear succession plans to protect the firm and its employees.

By treating succession like a phased project plan, they ensure the firm's legacy endures.

Common Mistakes Architects Make in Estate Planning

- **Procrastination:** Architects are busy — but delay can be costly.
- **Failure to Update Documents:** Your life and assets change; your plan must evolve.
- **Ignoring Business Interests:** Your firm is likely one of your largest assets.
- **Neglecting Digital Assets:** Plans must include access to email, cloud files, client data.

Action Steps: Your Estate Planning Blueprint

1. **Inventory Your Assets:** List everything — real estate, savings, business interests, digital assets.
2. **Set Goals:** What do you want to happen to your assets? Who do you want to benefit?
3. **Hire Professionals:** Estate planning attorney, CPA, financial advisor.
4. **Draft Core Documents:** Will, trust (if needed), power of attorney, health care directive.
5. **Plan for Your Business:** Succession or sale strategy.
6. **Communicate:** Let your family know your plans.
7. **Review Regularly:** Reassess every 3–5 years or after major life changes.

Estate Planning for Different Life Stages

Young Architect (20s-30s):

- Basic will.
- Durable and health care POA.

- Start a retirement plan.

Mid-Career Architect (40s-50s):

- Revocable living trust.
- Update beneficiaries.
- Business succession framework.

Late Career Architect (60+):

- Advanced tax planning.
- Trust funding.
- Finalize business succession.

Key Takeaways

- Estate planning is about control, not just wealth.
- Every architect needs a will and power of attorney.
- Business owners need a succession plan as much as a design plan.
- Planning early gives you the most options.

Encouragement

You are more capable than you think — and you're building a future you can be proud of. Financial planning isn't about being perfect — it's about laying the groundwork and refining it over time. The smartest architects don't just design beautiful buildings — they design sustainable lives.

Review and revise your financial blueprint regularly, just like you'd update a set of construction documents.

Final Note

This isn't just about managing dollars.

It's about freedom, creativity, and security.

It's about protecting the wealth you work so hard to earn.

Maximizing your income without losing sight of balance and meaning.

Architecting a life that is structurally sound, aesthetically pleasing, and personally fulfilling.

It's about:

Owning your financial foundation.

Owning your trajectory.

Owning your life's design.

Worksheets and Checklists

Estate Planning Quick Checklist:

- Create or update your will.
- Set up a trust if necessary.
- Assign a durable power of attorney.
- Draft a living will and health care POA.
- Plan for your business succession.
- Review beneficiary designations.
- Organize digital asset access.
- Meet with an estate planning attorney.
- Review every 3–5 years.

Questions to Ask an Estate Planning Attorney:

- What kind of trust structure do you recommend for my situation?
- How can I minimize estate taxes?
- What happens to my firm if I pass away unexpectedly?
- How do I protect digital assets and intellectual property?

- What's the process for updating documents?

Digital Asset Inventory Template:

- Email accounts:
- Online banking:
- Cloud storage:
- Client/project files:
- Architectural licenses/certifications:
- Social media accounts:
- Intellectual property (plans, blueprints, designs):

Family Conversation Starters:

- "I want to make sure everything is clear for the future — can we discuss my estate plan?"
- "Here's where you'll find important documents if something happens."
- "I'd like your input on selecting a guardian for [child's name]."

Chapter 24: Succession Planning

Introduction: Why Succession Planning Matters for Architects

Architecture is a profession built on legacy. Every building, every space designed, and every firm built is a testament to the architect's vision and years of dedication. Yet, as with any carefully designed structure, if the foundation for the future isn't set, the risk of collapse increases.

Succession planning is about more than retirement; it is about protecting your life's work and ensuring that what you built endures beyond your direct involvement. For solo practitioners, it means ensuring your practice doesn't dissolve when you decide to step away. For partners in a firm, it means protecting the firm's value, legacy, and clients. Done correctly, succession planning offers financial security, preserves your professional legacy, and ensures continuity for your staff and clients.

Architects, known for being forward thinkers in design, must apply that same foresight to their professional lives. Planning for an exit or transition isn't admitting defeat; it's laying the groundwork for lasting impact.

Understanding Succession Planning

Succession planning refers to the strategic process of identifying, training, and preparing individuals to take over leadership roles and ownership responsibilities. It is about building a bridge from the present to the future.

For an architectural practice, succession planning typically encompasses:

- Transferring leadership to junior partners or new leadership.
- Selling the firm to another company.
- Transitioning to an Employee Stock Ownership Plan (ESOP).
- Merging with another firm.
- Liquidating assets and closing the firm.

Each option carries significant financial, legal, and emotional considerations.

Succession planning should begin years—even decades—before the intended transition. It's not just a retirement decision; it's a business strategy.

Key Elements of a Succession Plan

Just as you wouldn't design a building without a comprehensive set of plans, you shouldn't attempt succession without detailed planning.

1. Define Your Goals

- When do you want to exit?
- How much do you need financially from the sale or transition?
- Do you want the firm to continue under your name?
- Is keeping the current team intact a priority?

2. Identify Successors

- Junior partners

- Existing senior staff
- External buyers
- Other firms

3. Value the Firm

- Business valuation is complex for architecture firms.
- Factors include revenue history, client lists, brand reputation, intellectual property (IP), and backlog of work.
- Hire a professional valuator familiar with service-based businesses.

4. Develop Training and Transition Plans

- Gradually transfer client relationships.
- Train successors on business operations.
- Transition leadership roles publicly.

5. Legal Structure and Documents

- Update shareholder agreements.
- Draft buy-sell agreements.
- Review contracts, leases, and vendor relationships.

6. Financial Planning

- Create projections for profitability post-transition.
- Ensure personal retirement plans align with succession proceeds.

7. Communication Plan

- Transparent conversations with staff.
- Communication with clients and vendors.
- Public announcements.

8. Timeline

- Create a timeline with key milestones.
- Adjust for unexpected delays.

Common Succession Planning Models

1. Internal Sale to Employees or Partners

Many architects prefer an internal sale to trusted employees. This approach often involves selling shares over time.

Pros:

- Maintains firm culture.
- Rewards loyal employees.
- Gradual financial payout.

Cons:

- May require seller financing.
- Risk if internal buyers lack management skills.

Steps:

- Establish clear criteria for ownership.
- Determine financing structure (seller notes, bank loans, profit-sharing).
- Gradually transfer control.

2. Merger with or Acquisition by Another Firm

Another path is merging with a larger firm or selling outright.

Pros:

- Immediate liquidity.
- Access to more resources for staff and clients.

Cons:

- Potential loss of culture and brand.
- Disruption for staff and clients.

Steps:

- Find the right cultural and operational fit.
- Engage M&A advisors.
- Structure the deal carefully (asset sale vs. stock sale).

3. Employee Stock Ownership Plan (ESOP)

An ESOP allows employees to buy the firm over time, typically using borrowed funds.

Pros:

- Provides an exit strategy.
- Motivates and retains staff.

Cons:

- Complex and expensive to set up.
- Requires firm profitability.

Steps:

- Hire ESOP consultants.
- Restructure firm to meet ESOP requirements.
- Transition leadership gradually.

4. Family Succession

Some architects pass the firm to children or relatives.

Pros:

- Keeps business in the family.

Cons:

- Family may not have the skills or interest.

Steps:

- Honestly assess interest and capability.
- Formalize transition and ownership plans.
- Address family dynamics openly.

5. Liquidation

In some cases, owners choose to close the firm.

Pros:

- Clean exit.

Cons:

- No ongoing legacy.

- Staff layoffs.

Steps:

- Notify clients and employees.
- Complete all active projects.
- Sell assets.

Valuing an Architecture Firm

Firm valuation is both art and science.

Key Factors:

- Revenue (especially recurring revenue)
- Profit margins
- Client base and backlog
- Reputation and brand
- Talent retention and leadership pipeline
- Contracts and IP (e.g., designs, models)
- Location and real estate assets

Valuation methods include:

- **Income Approach:** Future earnings discounted to present value.
- **Market Approach:** Comparing to recent sales of similar firms.
- **Asset Approach:** Valuing tangible and intangible assets.

It is crucial to hire valuation professionals who understand architecture firms' unique nature as professional service businesses.

Financial Considerations

Succession affects personal and firm finances.

For the Firm:

- Ensure the firm has healthy cash flow.
- Review debt obligations.
- Analyze ongoing project risks.

For the Owner:

- Confirm how succession funds fit into personal retirement plans.
- Consider tax implications.
- Diversify investments to avoid overreliance on the firm's future success.

Legal Considerations

Key Documents:

- Shareholder Agreements.
- Buy-Sell Agreements.
- Non-Compete and Non-Solicit Clauses.
- Employment Contracts.
- Client Contracts.

Work closely with attorneys experienced in professional services to avoid costly mistakes.

Emotional and Cultural Considerations

Selling or transitioning a firm is emotional. It's your legacy, your life's work.

- **Identity:** Architects often intertwine their identity with their practice.
- **Culture:** Will the firm's culture survive the transition?
- **Relationships:** Long-standing client relationships require careful handoff.

Prepare yourself and your team emotionally. Provide mentorship and support throughout the process.

Real-World Scenarios

Scenario 1: The Internal Buyout

John, a solo practitioner, started his firm 30 years ago. He identified two senior associates interested in ownership. Over five years, he sold 10% equity per year while mentoring them on leadership, operations, and client management. Upon retirement, the transition was seamless.

Scenario 2: Merger Success

Samantha's mid-size firm merged with a larger multidisciplinary firm. She received a lump sum payment and continued as a consultant during the transition. Her team gained access to bigger projects, and the firm's legacy lived on.

Scenario 3: The Failed Plan

David delayed succession planning. When he decided to retire, no internal candidates were ready, and a merger fell through. He liquidated assets and closed the firm. His staff scattered, and clients moved on.

Lesson: Start planning early.

Action Steps: Start Today

1. **Self-Assessment:** Where do you stand?
2. **Timeline:** Draft a 5-10 year succession timeline.
3. **Identify Successors:** Start conversations.
4. **Business Valuation:** Schedule a professional appraisal.
5. **Financial Review:** Meet with a CPA and financial advisor.
6. **Legal Prep:** Consult an attorney.
7. **Communication Plan:** Start planning how to tell clients and staff.
8. **Training:** Begin leadership development.
9. **Backup Plan:** Plan for unexpected illness or death.
10. **Regular Reviews:** Revisit your succession plan annually.

Plain Language Breakdown

Buy-Sell Agreement: A contract dictating how a partner's share of a business may be reassigned if that partner dies or leaves.

Valuation: The process of estimating the worth of your firm.

ESOP: Employee Stock Ownership Plan — a program that provides a firm's workforce with an ownership interest in the company.

Exit Strategy: A plan for how you will eventually leave the firm.

Successor: The person(s) who will take over your firm.

Encouragement

Succession planning is a sign of strength, not weakness. You have the tools, the vision, and the capacity to architect not just buildings but your professional legacy. By planning thoughtfully and acting early, you are not just protecting your financial future; you are extending your creative and professional influence for generations to come.

Reminder

Financial planning, like design, is iterative. You refine, adjust, and evolve as circumstances change. Your succession plan should be a living document, reviewed annually and updated as necessary.

Takeaway

The smartest architects don't just design beautiful buildings—they design sustainable, thriving practices. Succession planning is your blueprint for long-term success.

Final Prompt

Set a calendar reminder now: Review and revise your financial blueprint annually, just like you'd update a set of construction documents.

Final Note

This chapter isn't about endings; it's about continuities. It's about freedom, creativity, and security. It's about:

- Owning your financial foundation.
- Owning your trajectory.
- Owning your life's design.

Succession planning is one more act of design—not of space or structure, but of the future itself.

Chapter 25: Phased Retirement — Building a Gradual Exit Strategy

The Concept of Phased Retirement

Phased retirement isn't just an HR buzzword; it's a smart, strategic bridge between the full-on intensity of a career in architecture and the flexibility of your later years. It allows seasoned professionals to gradually step back, rediscover passions, and stay financially active without the pressures of managing full-time projects.

For architects, whose work is deeply tied to identity, purpose, and creativity, walking away entirely at 65 isn't always the right answer. Instead, phased retirement creates a graceful off-ramp. It offers you a way to leverage your expertise through consulting, mentoring, or teaching, while easing financial strain by maintaining some income.

Why Architects Should Consider Phased Retirement

Architecture is unique. It's not just a job; it's a craft, a legacy. Phased retirement allows you to protect your health and enjoy more leisure while continuing to exercise your design muscles and problem-solving skills.

Moreover, architecture demands a long runway to mastery. Clients, firms, and academic institutions value that wisdom. You become a resource, a mentor, a sounding board for complex problems—and you get compensated for it.

And let's not forget: financially, phased retirement can be the difference between drawing down your savings early and letting them grow a few more years.

Consulting: Your Expertise, Your Terms

Consulting is one of the most popular avenues for phased retirement. Firms hire experienced architects to:

- Guide complex projects.
- Advise on design reviews.
- Help mentor junior staff.
- Provide strategic oversight without a day-to-day commitment.

Setting Up Your Consulting Practice

Treat it like a business. Even if you consult just part-time, you should:

- Set up a simple LLC for liability protection and tax advantages.
- Open a business banking account.
- Track expenses (travel, home office, software subscriptions) for deductions.
- Consider professional liability insurance.

Financial Implications

Consulting income can be significant. Depending on your workload, it might allow you to delay claiming Social Security, boost your retirement savings, or cover healthcare premiums before Medicare eligibility.

But remember: consulting income is self-employment income. You'll need to:

- Pay estimated taxes quarterly.
- Cover both sides of Social Security and Medicare (15.3% self-employment tax).
- Set aside funds for retirement via a SEP IRA or Solo 401(k).

Teaching: Inspiring the Next Generation

If you've ever thought about teaching, phased retirement is your chance. Universities, community colleges, and even high schools seek experienced architects.

- Adjunct professor roles are typically part-time.
- Guest lecturing and critiques are short-term and flexible.

Benefits:

- Staying intellectually active.
- Expanding your network.
- Supplementing your income without the demands of private practice.

Financially, adjunct positions usually pay per class or credit hour. It's not "retire rich" money, but it's steady, and some institutions offer health insurance for adjuncts teaching above a certain threshold.

Mentoring: Legacy Beyond Buildings

Many architects find immense satisfaction in mentoring young designers. This can happen formally, through:

- AIA mentorship programs.
- University alumni networks.
- Firm leadership training.

Or informally:

- Lunches with junior colleagues.
- Portfolio reviews.
- Speaking engagements.

Mentoring might not always pay directly, but it enhances your reputation and opens doors for consulting or part-time gigs. Plus, it adds meaning and continuity to your career.

Financial Planning for Part-Time Retirement Work

Even part-time income affects your retirement plan. Let's break it down:

- **Social Security Timing**: If you earn above a certain limit before full retirement age, your benefits can be temporarily reduced.
- **Tax Brackets**: Part-time work could push you into a higher tax bracket, so plan with your CPA.
- **Healthcare**: Pre-Medicare retirees need a plan. Consulting and teaching rarely come with benefits, so you'll need to budget for private insurance or COBRA.
- **Retirement Contributions**: Keep funding your retirement accounts if possible. SEP IRAs and Solo 401(k)s allow large catch-up contributions.

Strategic Benefits of Phased Retirement

Beyond income, phased retirement offers:

- Mental stimulation.
- Professional relevance.
- Flexibility to travel, pursue hobbies, and spend time with family.
- A softer financial landing pad that extends the longevity of your portfolio.

Planning Your Phased Retirement Timeline

Start planning five to ten years before you want to wind down:

1. **Audit Your Finances**: Know your numbers—expenses, retirement balances, healthcare costs.
2. **Visualize Your Workload**: How many hours a week? What types of projects or roles appeal to you?
3. **Network Proactively**: Let colleagues know you're available for consulting or teaching.
4. **Upskill if Necessary**: Software evolves. Teaching requires different skills. Prepare.
5. **Plan for Downtime**: Be realistic—work might not be consistent at first.

Pros and Cons of Phased Retirement

Pros

- Continued income.
- Intellectual engagement.
- Opportunity to mentor and give back.
- Flexibility.

Cons

- Inconsistent workload.
- Self-employment taxes.
- Need to secure your own benefits.
- Potentially complex financial planning.

Real-World Scenario: Michael's Transition

Michael spent 35 years designing civic buildings. He wasn't ready to stop cold turkey. At 62, he:

- Began teaching one studio course per semester.
- Consulted for his old firm on design competitions.
- Took summer trips with his spouse.

His consulting brought in $50,000 a year. His teaching added another $15,000. He delayed Social Security until 70, maximized his Solo 401(k), and stayed intellectually and socially engaged.

Action Steps to Launch Your Phased Retirement

- **Talk to a Financial Advisor**: Model different scenarios.
- **Set Up a Business Entity**: Even if it's small.
- **Update Your Resume**: Highlight your expertise.
- **Reconnect with Old Colleagues**: Opportunities often come through your network.

- **Budget Conservatively**: Assume lean years early on.

Common Mistakes to Avoid

- Underestimating healthcare costs.
- Not paying quarterly estimated taxes.
- Overcommitting and burning out.
- Neglecting to market yourself.

Building Social Capital for Long-Term Success

Your network is your biggest asset. Stay involved in AIA chapters, alumni associations, and industry events. Share your knowledge generously—it'll pay dividends.

Tax Optimization Strategies

- Max out your Solo 401(k) or SEP IRA contributions.
- Deduct home office expenses.
- Track and deduct business expenses like software, travel, and professional dues.
- Consider a defined benefit plan if your consulting income is significant.

Balancing Work and Leisure

Resist the urge to say "yes" to every opportunity. One of the key benefits of phased retirement is control—use it. Set boundaries around your time.

Teaching and Mentoring: Not Just for Income

Teaching and mentoring fill a gap that money alone can't. They offer:

- Personal fulfillment.
- Legacy building.
- Networking expansion.
- Intellectual stimulation.

Plus, schools often value professional experience highly, sometimes even over academic credentials.

Consulting Contracts: What to Watch For

- Scope of work.
- Hourly or project-based rates.
- Payment terms.
- Liability clauses.

Consult a contracts attorney for larger projects.

Healthcare Strategies Before 65

- COBRA coverage (expensive but reliable).
- ACA marketplace plans (subsidies might be available).
- Health-sharing ministries (low cost but limited coverage).

Maintaining Licensure

Even in phased retirement, maintaining your license boosts credibility. Plus, it may be required for certain consulting or teaching roles.

Stay current by:

- Completing CEUs.
- Renewing annually.
- Keeping professional insurance active if consulting.

Redefining Success

Phased retirement isn't "winding down." It's transitioning to a new kind of professional success—one with more control, more flexibility, and often, more meaning.

You Are Still an Architect

Remember, titles may change, workloads may decrease, but your identity as an architect endures. Your wisdom is your value.

A Moment of Encouragement

You are more capable than you think. You're not stepping back—you're building the next phase of a thoughtful, intentional life. Phased retirement isn't an end. It's a masterfully designed transition.

A Reminder

Financial planning isn't about being perfect. It's about being prepared, structured, and adaptable—like the best design projects.

A Clear Takeaway

The smartest architects don't just design beautiful buildings—they design sustainable, fulfilling lives.

A Subtle Prompt

Review and revise your financial blueprint regularly, just like you'd update a set of construction documents. Phased retirement deserves the same level of attention and care as your most detailed design.

Chapter 26: Healthcare and Long-Term Care Planning

Healthcare costs have become one of the most critical concerns for architects approaching retirement. Even the most carefully constructed financial plan can crack under the strain of unexpected medical expenses. As you design your financial blueprint, healthcare and long-term care should be foundational considerations—because they are not optional and, without proper planning, can become catastrophic.

Medicare: The Basics

When you hit age 65, Medicare becomes a central component of your healthcare coverage—but it's not as simple as enrolling and forgetting. Medicare comes in parts: Part A (Hospital Insurance) generally covers inpatient care and is usually premium-free if you or your spouse paid Medicare taxes while working. Part B (Medical Insurance) covers outpatient care and doctor visits but comes with a monthly premium, which is adjusted based on income.

Part C (Medicare Advantage) combines Part A, Part B, and often Part D (prescription drug coverage) into a single plan offered by private insurers. Part D is optional, but if you delay enrollment without other creditable drug coverage, you could face lifelong penalties.

Key Medicare Considerations for Architects:

- **Timing**: If you're still working and covered by an employer's plan at

65, you might delay Part B to avoid unnecessary premiums.

- **Gaps in Coverage**: Original Medicare does not cover dental, vision, hearing, or long-term care. Medigap plans (supplemental policies) can help fill some gaps.
- **Income-Related Adjustments**: High-income retirees could face surcharges (IRMAA) on their Medicare premiums.

Health Savings Accounts (HSAs)

If you have access to a Health Savings Account during your working years—typically through a high-deductible health plan (HDHP)—you're sitting on a powerful retirement healthcare tool. HSAs offer triple tax advantages:

- Contributions are tax-deductible.
- Growth is tax-free.
- Withdrawals for qualified medical expenses are tax-free.

Even better, after age 65, withdrawals for non-medical expenses are taxed as ordinary income—essentially converting the HSA into a "stealth" IRA if needed.

For architects with inconsistent income (think solo practitioners), an HSA can be an efficient way to manage variable cash flow while saving aggressively for future healthcare expenses.

Healthcare Costs in Retirement

According to Fidelity's 2024 Retiree Health Care Cost Estimate, an average retired couple may need approximately $315,000 for medical expenses in retirement. That figure excludes long-term care, dental, and over-the-counter expenses.

Key healthcare costs to budget for:

- Medicare premiums and out-of-pocket costs.
- Prescription drugs.
- Dental, vision, and hearing care.

- Potential Medigap or Medicare Advantage plan premiums.
- Out-of-pocket maximums (especially if you stick with high-deductible plans).

Long-Term Care (LTC) Considerations

Few topics make people more uncomfortable than thinking about long-term care needs. Yet, statistically, 70% of people turning 65 today will need some form of long-term care.

Long-term care isn't just nursing home care. It includes assisted living, in-home health aides, and adult day care—none of which are covered by Medicare.

Options for Funding Long-Term Care:

1. **Self-Insurance**: Some architects with robust portfolios choose to earmark a portion of their assets to cover future long-term care needs.
2. **Long-Term Care Insurance (LTCI)**:

- Traditional LTCI policies pay a daily benefit for care, but premiums can be expensive and are subject to increase.
- Newer hybrid policies combine LTC benefits with life insurance or annuities—if you never use the LTC benefit, your heirs receive a death benefit.

1. **Life Insurance with LTC Riders**: Permanent life insurance policies can sometimes be augmented with long-term care riders, offering flexibility.
2. **Medicaid Planning**: Medicaid is the largest payer of long-term care costs, but you must meet strict income and asset requirements. Proactive planning (like trusts) can help preserve assets if you may need to qualify for Medicaid later.

Pros and Cons

HSAs

- Pros: Triple tax advantage, portability, flexible withdrawal.
- Cons: Requires HDHP; contribution limits are relatively low.

Medicare

- Pros: Predictable costs, wide availability.
- Cons: Limited coverage; premiums can be high for high-income earners.

Long-Term Care Insurance

- Pros: Provides dedicated funding; protects retirement assets.
- Cons: High cost; potential for premium increases.

Self-Insurance for LTC

- Pros: Flexibility; no premiums.
- Cons: Risk of depleting retirement funds; unpredictability.

Action Steps

1. **Start HSA Contributions Early**: Maximize your contributions while eligible.
2. **Estimate Retirement Healthcare Costs**: Work with a financial planner to build realistic models.
3. **Review Medicare Options Annually**: Plans and premiums can change; don't "set and forget."
4. **Evaluate LTC Insurance Early**: Premiums are cheaper the younger and healthier you are.
5. **Incorporate Healthcare into Your Retirement Income Plan**: Don't treat it as an afterthought.
6. **Consider a Hybrid LTC Policy**: If you're concerned about "use it or lose it" with traditional LTCI.

7. **Plan for Dental, Vision, and Hearing Costs Separately**: Use HSAs or personal savings.

Plain Language Breakdowns

Medicare vs. Medigap vs. Medicare Advantage:

Think of Original Medicare as the "core." Medigap fills in the cracks (copayments, deductibles). Medicare Advantage is an alternate core—a "bundled" private version.

HSA vs. FSA:

An HSA stays with you; it's yours forever and can grow. An FSA (Flexible Spending Account) is "use it or lose it."

Real-World Scenarios

1. **Sophia, 62, Principal Architect**:
2. Sophia's firm offers a high-deductible plan with an HSA. She's been maxing out her HSA, investing the funds, and plans to use it tax-free for Medicare premiums later.
3. **Mark, 66, Retired Solo Practitioner**:
4. Mark delayed Medicare Part B because he stayed on his wife's employer health plan. When she retires, they'll both need to enroll during a Special Enrollment Period.
5. **Denise, 70, Firm Founder**:
6. Denise bought a hybrid LTC-life insurance policy at age 55. She has peace of mind knowing that either she'll use the benefit for care or leave a legacy.

Structure Matters

As architects appreciate, good design solves problems before they arise. Healthcare and long-term care planning is no different. It's not just about today's premiums—it's about future-proofing your financial life.

- Start early.
- Revisit your plan annually.

- Integrate healthcare into your broader retirement and estate planning.

Education

Understand:

- How Medicare works and what it doesn't cover.
- The triple tax advantage of HSAs.
- The real risks of long-term care costs and how to mitigate them.

Empowerment

You've built a career on strong foundations. Now build a healthcare plan that's as resilient as the structures you've designed.

Engagement

Financial planning for healthcare isn't a chore—it's an extension of the thoughtful, careful approach you bring to every project.

End of Chapter Encouragement

You are more capable than you think. A solid healthcare and long-term care plan ensures that your financial blueprint is as structurally sound as your best work.

Financial planning isn't about being perfect. It's about laying the groundwork and refining it over time.

The smartest architects don't just design beautiful buildings—they design sustainable lives.

Subtle Prompt

Review and revise your healthcare and long-term care blueprint annually, just like you'd update a set of construction documents.

Final Note

This chapter isn't just about managing healthcare costs. It's about ensuring your freedom, creativity, and security in the years ahead.

It's about:

- Owning your financial foundation.
- Owning your trajectory.

- Owning your life's design.

Chapter 27: Social Security and Pension Considerations

Understanding the Financial Structures You Need for Retirement

Why Social Security and Pensions Matter

As an architect, you are trained to anticipate future needs in every structure you design. Retirement is no different. The structure you are designing is not made of steel and glass but of time, money, and choices. Social Security and pensions are the load-bearing walls of many architects' retirement plans. Understanding how they work, when to claim them, and how to incorporate them into your larger financial blueprint is essential to achieving a structurally sound retirement.

Social Security: The Basics

Social Security was designed as a safety net. While it's unlikely to cover all your expenses in retirement, it plays a crucial role in providing a steady, guaranteed income. For many, it's the only source of inflation-adjusted income that lasts for life.

How It Works

Your Social Security benefits are based on your 35 highest-earning years. If you work fewer than 35 years, zeros are averaged in. As an architect, your career might have periods of self-employment, high-income years, or slow periods. Each impacts your eventual benefit.

The age at which you claim Social Security affects how much you receive:

- Early retirement (as early as age 62) reduces your benefit.

- Full retirement age (FRA) is between 66 and 67, depending on your birth year.
- Delaying beyond your FRA up to age 70 increases your benefit by about 8% per year.

Pros and Cons of Early vs. Delayed Claims

Pros of Claiming Early:

- Immediate income.
- Useful if you have health issues or a shorter life expectancy.

Cons of Claiming Early:

- Reduced monthly benefits permanently.
- Lower survivor benefits for your spouse.

Pros of Delaying:

- Higher monthly income for life.
- Increased survivor benefits.

Cons of Delaying:

- Requires using other savings or continuing to work.

Action Steps:

- Request your Social Security Statement at ssa.gov.
- Estimate benefits at different claiming ages.
- Factor Social Security into your broader retirement income plan.

Understanding the Earnings Test

If you claim Social Security before your FRA and continue to work, you may be subject to the "earnings test." In 2024, for example, $1 in benefits is withheld for every $2 you earn above $21,240. After reaching FRA, this penalty disappears.

Spousal and Survivor Benefits

Even if your spouse never worked, they can claim a benefit based on your work history. Similarly, if you pass away, your spouse may be entitled to survivor benefits, often the higher of your two benefits.

Maximizing Benefits for Married Architects

Coordinating benefits between spouses can maximize your household income. For example:

- One spouse claims early; the other delays to increase the survivor benefit.
- Both delay to maximize income.

Understanding Pensions for Architects

Pensions, once common, are now a rarity in the private sector but still exist in government, academia, and some large firms. As an architect, you may encounter:

- Defined Benefit Plans (traditional pensions).
- Defined Contribution Plans (401(k), 403(b), etc.).

Defined Benefit Plans

These plans promise a specific monthly benefit based on salary and years of service.

Key Elements:

- Vesting period: How long you must work to earn benefits.
- Benefit formula: Often a percentage of average salary times years worked.
- Early retirement options: Benefits may be reduced if taken before a certain age.

Action Steps:

- Request a pension summary from HR.
- Understand your benefit calculation.
- Factor in survivorship options.

Defined Contribution Plans

While not a pension in the traditional sense, your 401(k) or 403(b) is a crucial retirement vehicle. You and your employer contribute, and you manage investments.

If You Worked in the Public Sector or Academia

Architects working for universities, government agencies, or nonprofit organizations may have:

- 403(b) Plans: Similar to 401(k)s but for nonprofits.
- 457(b) Plans: Additional deferred compensation plans.
- State pension plans: Common in public universities and government.

Public Pensions and the Windfall Elimination Provision (WEP)

If you worked in a job not covered by Social Security (some state or local government roles) and qualify for a pension, the WEP may reduce your Social Security benefit.

The Government Pension Offset (GPO) may also reduce spousal or survivor benefits.

Action Steps:

- If applicable, check if WEP or GPO affects you.
- Use the SSA's WEP calculator.

When Should You Claim Social Security?

There's no one-size-fits-all answer. Consider:

- Health and family longevity.

- Need for income.
- Whether you're still working.
- Spousal benefit coordination.

Case Study: Architect at 62 vs. 70

Emma, a 62-year-old architect, has the option to claim $1,500/month now or $2,640/month at age 70.

If Emma claims early:

- Receives $1,500 x 12 = $18,000 per year.
- Over eight years, she would collect $144,000 before she could claim $2,640.

If she lives past her early 80s, waiting would yield greater lifetime income.

Pensions and Social Security Together

Coordinating pensions and Social Security is key:

- Know when your pension starts.
- Compare lump sum vs. annuity options.
- Assess survivor benefits.
- Understand tax implications.

Tax Considerations

Social Security can be taxable based on your "provisional income" (AGI + nontaxable interest + 50% of Social Security benefits).

- Below $25,000 (single) or $32,000 (married): No taxes on benefits.
- Up to 85% of benefits taxable at higher income levels.

Pension income is generally fully taxable at ordinary income rates.

Strategies for Reducing Taxes:

- Roth IRA conversions.

- Managing withdrawals from different account types.
- Delaying Social Security to lower provisional income.

Building a Financial Blueprint

Think of your retirement income like a well-integrated building system:

- Foundation: Social Security and pension income.
- Structure: 401(k), IRA, brokerage accounts.
- Finishing materials: Part-time work, real estate income.

Diversifying Income Sources

Relying solely on Social Security is risky. A mix of pension, retirement savings, and personal investments creates stability.

Contingency Planning

Just as architects plan for structural redundancies, you should plan for financial "what-ifs."

- What if Social Security benefits are reduced?
- What if pension funding becomes an issue?

Diversification and conservative withdrawal rates can provide security.

Part-Time Work and Social Security

Working after claiming Social Security can impact your benefit if under FRA. But it also has positives:

- Additional income.
- Potential for delaying retirement savings withdrawals.
- Social engagement and mental stimulation.

Long-Term Care Planning

Long-term care can deplete retirement savings. Consider:

- Long-term care insurance.

- Hybrid life/long-term care policies.
- Self-insuring with savings.

Estate Planning

Ensure you have:

- Updated beneficiaries.
- A will.
- Durable power of attorney.
- Healthcare proxy.

Leaving a Legacy

If you own part of a firm, consider succession planning:

- Sell to a partner.
- Transition to employee ownership.
- Merge with another firm.

These decisions affect your retirement security and your firm's future.

Final Thoughts: Architecting a Secure Future

Your career has been about thoughtful planning, precise execution, and balancing form and function. Your retirement plan should reflect the same principles.

Social Security and pensions are vital, but they're not the entire blueprint. Understand them. Respect their strengths and limitations. Integrate them with other financial elements.

Financial planning is not about guessing the future — it's about preparing for it thoughtfully, just as you do with every project you've designed.

A Moment of Encouragement

You are more capable than you think. You've spent your life building dreams for others. Now it's time to build a secure, fulfilling retirement for yourself.

A Reminder

Financial planning isn't about perfection. It's about laying a good foundation and making thoughtful adjustments over time.

A Clear Takeaway

The smartest architects don't just design beautiful buildings — they design sustainable lives.

A Subtle Prompt

Review and revise your financial blueprint regularly, just like you'd update a set of construction documents.

Final Note

This chapter isn't just about Social Security and pensions. It's about freedom, creativity, and security.

It's about:

- Protecting the wealth you've worked so hard to build.
- Maximizing your income without losing sight of balance and meaning.
- Architecting a life that is structurally sound, aesthetically pleasing, and personally fulfilling.

Own your financial foundation.

Own your trajectory.

Own your life's design.

Chapter 28: Building a Retirement Lifestyle Budget

For architects, planning a building is second nature. You consider load-bearing walls, mechanical systems, egress routes, and flow. Your design is precise because the success of the structure depends on your diligence.

Planning your retirement lifestyle should be no different.

You've spent decades designing buildings for others. Now it's time to design your future life—one that's sustainable, functional, and fulfilling. But to build that, you need a realistic blueprint: a retirement lifestyle budget.

Let's walk through it together.

The Foundation: Understanding Your Retirement Income

Your retirement budget begins with income. Before you talk about expenses, you need to understand how much money you'll have coming in.

Think of income sources as structural columns holding up your retirement plan:

- **Social Security**: Estimate your benefits based on your work history and claiming age.
- **Pensions**: If you've worked in public or academic settings, calculate what you're eligible for.

- **Retirement Savings**: 401(k)s, IRAs, brokerage accounts, and annuities.
- **Rental Income**: Properties you may own and lease.
- **Consulting or Part-Time Work**: If you plan to stay partially active in your profession.

Project conservative income assumptions. Assume modest growth and factor in taxes—your withdrawals from tax-deferred accounts will be taxable.

Designing for Sustainability: Estimating Retirement Expenses

Your retirement lifestyle budget must be realistic and comprehensive. Sketch out a "needs vs. wants" diagram:

- **Fixed Necessities**:
- Housing (mortgage, rent, taxes, maintenance)
- Utilities (electric, water, gas, internet)
- Food
- Transportation (car payments, insurance, maintenance)
- Health insurance and out-of-pocket medical costs
- **Variable Necessities**:
- Clothing
- Home maintenance and repairs
- Personal care
- **Lifestyle Desires**:
- Travel
- Dining out
- Hobbies
- Entertainment
- Gifts and philanthropy
- **Surprises**:
- Home renovations

- Family emergencies
- Economic downturns

The goal is to calculate a monthly "retirement paycheck" you can live on comfortably.

The Risk of Exhausting Savings

The biggest fear in retirement isn't boredom—it's running out of money.

Architects, like many professionals, tend to have longer life expectancies due to education and income levels. Planning to age 90 is conservative; planning to 95 is safer.

Use the "4% Rule" as a rough guide: withdraw no more than 4% of your retirement savings annually, adjusted for inflation. But recognize the rule's limitations—market volatility, healthcare shocks, and longer lives can disrupt it.

Create a "stress test" budget:

- What if the market has a 20% downturn in the first five years?
- What if you live to 100?
- What if healthcare costs double?

Good designs plan for the worst while hoping for the best.

Downsizing or Relocating: Strategic Considerations

Your biggest expense—and biggest opportunity—is housing.

Downsizing

Selling a large, expensive home and moving to a smaller, more efficient space can free up significant capital.

Pros:

- Lower property taxes

- Less maintenance
- Cash infusion from home sale

Cons:

- Emotional attachment to your home
- Moving costs
- Smaller space may limit hosting family or hobbies

Relocating

Some retirees move to areas with lower costs of living, better climate, or proximity to family.

Pros:

- Lower taxes
- Lower cost of living
- Better access to healthcare or community activities

Cons:

- Leaving a familiar community
- Travel costs to visit friends/family
- Possible higher healthcare costs depending on location

Carefully weigh:

- State income taxes
- Estate/inheritance taxes
- Sales and property taxes
- Healthcare infrastructure

Remember: where you live impacts not only your budget but your happiness.

Healthcare: Your Largest Wildcard

Even with Medicare, healthcare costs can be a budget-buster.

Plan for:

- Medicare Part B and D premiums
- Medigap or Medicare Advantage premiums
- Out-of-pocket expenses
- Dental, vision, and hearing care (not covered by Medicare)
- Long-term care insurance or costs

A Health Savings Account (HSA), if you have one, can be a valuable tool. Funds can be withdrawn tax-free for medical expenses.

Expect to spend at least $300,000 on healthcare over the course of retirement.

Building Flexibility Into Your Retirement Budget

Rigid budgets break under pressure. Flexible budgets bend and absorb shocks.

Build in:

- Discretionary spending leeway
- Emergency funds (even in retirement)
- Inflation adjustments (3% annually is a safe bet)
- A "bucket strategy"—divide your savings into short-term, medium-term, and long-term buckets

Think like an architect—plan for thermal expansion and material stress.

Action Steps for Building Your Retirement Lifestyle Budget

1. **Inventory Income Sources**: Calculate conservative estimates.
2. **Estimate Expenses**: Needs, wants, and surprises.
3. **Stress Test**: Model bad scenarios.
4. **Housing Plan**: Stay, downsize, or relocate?
5. **Healthcare Budget**: Account for rising costs.
6. **Flexibility**: Build room to adapt.
7. **Professional Help**: A fee-only financial planner can help align your retirement budget with your goals.

Real-World Story

"I always dreamed of retiring to a cabin by the lake," says Jennifer, a 62-year-old architect. "But when I ran the numbers, maintaining that property would have eaten up a third of my retirement income. Instead, I bought a condo downtown—smaller, maintenance-free, and walkable to everything I love. I still visit the lake—but as a vacation rental guest, not an owner."

Jennifer's story underscores the principle: Lifestyle planning is about priorities and trade-offs.

Final Thoughts

Just as every project you've ever designed needed a budget, timeline, and blueprint, so too does your retirement.

The smartest architects don't just plan the building—they plan for how it will stand the test of time.

You have the tools. You have the discipline. You have the vision.

Now, design your most important project yet: a life that reflects the best of what you've built—and lets you enjoy it without fear of running out of time or money.

"You are more capable than you think—and you're building a future you can be proud of."

Financial planning isn't about being perfect—it's about laying the groundwork and refining it over time.

The smartest architects don't just design beautiful buildings—they design sustainable lives.

Review and revise your financial blueprint regularly, just like you'd update a set of construction documents.

Own your financial foundation.

Own your trajectory.

Own your life's design.

Part V: Special Considerations — Financial Literacy Unique to Architects

Architecture is more than a profession — it's a lifestyle, a calling, and often a long-term passion project. But with this unique career path come financial challenges and opportunities that differ from many other fields. Part V addresses these complexities head-on, giving architects a tailored approach to financial literacy that respects the nuances of their work, education, career trajectories, and personal ambitions.

In this section, we dive deep into the distinct financial realities architects face: extended educational timelines, delayed earning potential, the costs and rewards of professional licensure, and the entrepreneurial spirit that often leads many to start their own firms. We'll unpack how the cyclical nature of the economy impacts project pipelines — and how to build a financial buffer that can weather the downturns.

Architects also bring a rare combination of creativity and pragmatism to their personal lives — a gift that, when properly channeled, can be a significant asset in building wealth, managing investments, and planning for long-term financial freedom. However, architects are often overlooked by traditional financial advice models that don't account for career-specific issues like fluctuating income, delayed retirement saving starts, or the financial risks of firm ownership.

This part covers specialized topics such as:

- How to structure compensation agreements when moving into senior or partner roles.

- Navigating the financial complexities of running a boutique or solo practice.
- Strategic considerations for architects involved in public sector work, academia, or consulting.
- Understanding how your design sensibility can sometimes lead to lifestyle inflation — and how to manage it wisely.
- Balancing personal real estate investments with professional ambitions.
- Building a succession plan that ensures your firm's legacy while protecting your personal financial future.
- The importance of maintaining professional liability insurance, even in semi-retirement.

We'll also explore how architects can turn their professional networks into financial assets, how to capitalize on their unique skill sets in consulting or teaching during phased retirement, and how to manage healthcare, long-term care, and insurance needs in ways that support — rather than restrict — a vibrant, purposeful second act.

By the end of this section, you'll be equipped with a blueprint — not just for career success, but for designing a life that is as thoughtfully constructed as the buildings and spaces you create.

Financial Literacy for Architects isn't about fitting into someone else's mold — it's about helping you build the life you envision, with clarity, control, and creativity.

Chapter 29: Creative vs Financial Tension

Navigating financial decisions without sacrificing creativity is one of the most persistent, yet least openly discussed, challenges architects face. As creatives, architects are driven by vision, aesthetics, innovation, and design principles that elevate human experience. But architecture is also a business. Whether you are working in a firm, running your own practice, or freelancing, your ability to manage finances thoughtfully while preserving the integrity of your work is crucial.

In this chapter, we explore the complex relationship between creativity and money, and how architects can reconcile the two to build not only beautiful spaces but also sustainable careers. We will also tackle the tough but necessary question: How do you price your creative labor fairly without feeling like you're "selling out"?

The Creative Calling vs. Financial Reality

Architecture has always been a profession rooted in both art and science, creativity and structure. Yet, for many architects, the romanticized vision of designing iconic structures clashes with the economic demands of running a practice or maintaining a steady career. This tension can cause stress, disillusionment, and even career burnout.

The key is not to view creativity and financial responsibility as opposing forces but as complementary elements that can coexist with careful planning and mindset shifts.

Understanding the Financial Undercurrents of Creative Work

Why Architects Undervalue Their Labor

- **Cultural Conditioning**: Architecture school emphasizes design quality and theory, often sidelining business and financial literacy.
- **Passion vs. Pay**: Many architects feel guilty charging for work they enjoy.
- **Fear of Losing Projects**: Especially early in their careers, architects underprice their services to secure projects and build portfolios.
- **Market Pressure**: Competition from firms and freelancers willing to work for less creates a "race to the bottom."

Awareness is the first step to overcoming these tendencies. Architects must recognize that their creative labor has real, quantifiable value.

Pricing Your Creative Labor Fairly

Start With Your Worth

To price your services fairly, you need to understand your worth. This means evaluating:

- **Your Experience**: Years in the field, certifications, specialized knowledge.
- **Your Value to Clients**: How your designs solve client problems, enhance property value, or impact communities.
- **Your Overhead**: Office expenses, software licenses, insurance, marketing, continuing education.
- **Your Desired Income**: What do you need to live comfortably, save, invest, and achieve your personal financial goals?

Pricing is part art, part science. Benchmark against industry standards, but don't undervalue what you bring to the table.

Hourly Rate vs. Fixed Fee

Both have pros and cons:

- **Hourly Rates**: Useful for smaller or more flexible projects, but clients may balk at the unknown total.
- **Fixed Fees**: Provide clients with predictability but require careful scoping.

Hybrid models—combining a fixed fee for defined services and hourly billing for extras—can provide balance.

Transparency and Confidence

Explain your pricing structure to clients confidently. Transparency builds trust. Be prepared to articulate why your fee is what it is, emphasizing the value clients receive, not just the cost.

Balancing Financial Prudence with Creative Freedom

The "Creative Tax" Myth

Many creatives believe that financial compromise is the price they must pay for freedom. This is a false dichotomy. Financial stability can enhance creativity by reducing stress and allowing greater focus on design.

Smart Project Selection

Choose projects that align with your creative goals and financial needs. Every project should be evaluated on:

- **Financial Viability**: Does it pay fairly?
- **Portfolio Potential**: Will it enhance your body of work?
- **Relationship Building**: Does it offer networking or future opportunity value?

Sometimes, it's strategic to take a lower-paying project if it meets other goals—but only if it's part of an overall balanced strategy.

Money as a Design Constraint

Architects are familiar with constraints: site conditions, zoning laws, material limitations. Money is simply another constraint to design around. Embracing financial parameters as part of the design process can foster greater innovation and discipline.

Building a Financially Sustainable Practice

Revenue Streams

Diversifying revenue can reduce dependence on a single type of project:

- **Consulting**: Design reviews, feasibility studies, expert witness work.
- **Teaching**: Adjunct professorships, workshops.
- **Product Design**: Furniture, lighting, modular systems.
- **Publishing**: Books, paid newsletters, speaking engagements.

Value-Based Fees

Move from time-based billing to value-based billing where appropriate. Charge based on the value you create, not just the hours you log.

Negotiating Without Fear

Negotiation is not confrontation. It's collaboration. Frame negotiations around mutual benefit and be ready to walk away from deals that don't honor your worth.

Case Studies: Navigating the Balance

Case Study 1: The Passion Project

An architect takes on a pro bono cultural center design. Though the project is unpaid, it earns significant press, awards, and leads to several high-paying commissions.

Case Study 2: The Lowball Trap

Another architect consistently underbids to win projects. Over time, this leads to burnout, resentment, and financial instability, forcing a career pivot.

Case Study 3: Strategic Diversification

A firm expands into product design, creating an additional revenue stream that supports the practice during lean periods without sacrificing design standards.

Action Steps for Architects

1. **Audit Your Financials**: Know your numbers—income, expenses, profit margins.
2. **Set Minimum Fees**: Never take on work below your minimum threshold.
3. **Practice Saying No**: Turn down projects that don't meet your financial and creative criteria.
4. **Learn to Negotiate**: Take courses, read books, practice.
5. **Invest in Financial Literacy**: Make ongoing financial education part of your professional development.

Mindset Shifts for Long-Term Success

- **See Yourself as a Professional**: You're not just an artist—you're a professional solving complex problems.
- **Money Is Not the Enemy**: Financial health supports creative freedom.
- **Pricing Is a Reflection of Value**: Charging fairly reflects respect for your work and the industry.

Conclusion

Creative work and financial stability are not mutually exclusive. They are complementary forces that, when balanced carefully, can elevate not only your career but also the quality and impact of your work.

As an architect, you already have the tools: problem-solving, design thinking, and systems analysis. Apply these same skills to your financial life.

Because the smartest architects don't just design beautiful buildings—they design sustainable lives.

And remember: Review and refine your financial blueprint regularly, just as you would revisit and revise a set of construction documents. It's the mark of a true master planner.

Would you like me to continue expanding this chapter to reach the full 10,000 words as outlined?

Chapter 30: Handling Inconsistent Income: Building Financial Stability in an Unpredictable Industry

Introduction: The Reality of Architectural Income

Architecture is a profession built on creativity, vision, and execution. Yet behind the stunning renderings and award-winning designs lies a practical reality many don't talk about enough: financial unpredictability. Particularly for freelance architects, small firm owners, and those who juggle project-based work, income can feel anything but steady.

It doesn't matter how talented you are or how respected your portfolio may be—feast-or-famine cycles are common. Some months, you're flush with client deposits and invoice payments. Other months, you're wondering if that proposal you sent out will ever get signed.

Inconsistent income isn't unique to architecture, but it has a special flavor in this industry. Long project timelines, delayed payments from clients, seasonal slowdowns, and reliance on economic cycles mean even the most seasoned professionals experience volatility.

So how do you, as an architect, design a financial plan that can withstand the ups and downs of your profession? How do you build a system that keeps your bills paid, your goals on track, and your stress levels manageable—even when your income isn't predictable?

This chapter offers a blueprint.

The Unique Income Challenges Architects Face

Before we dive into the solutions, let's examine the specific income issues architects face:

1. Project-Based Revenue

Unlike salaried employees, freelance architects or small firm owners get paid by the project. Payment schedules vary: some clients pay a retainer upfront and installments over time; others delay final payment until a project milestone is reached or the job is finished.

This creates natural gaps in cash flow between project phases, especially if projects are delayed.

2. Long Payment Cycles

Clients—especially larger organizations—may take 30, 60, or even 90 days to pay an invoice. Even when you've done your part promptly, you can find yourself waiting months for compensation.

3. Economic Sensitivity

Architecture is tied closely to broader economic health. When the economy dips, construction slows, development projects get shelved, and architects see fewer job opportunities and client commissions.

4. Seasonality

Certain times of the year—like the winter holidays or summer months—can bring fewer client meetings and new projects, resulting in quieter income periods.

5. Scope Creep and Unpaid Labor

Projects can easily grow beyond their original scope. If you aren't vigilant about contract terms and change orders, you may find yourself doing extra work without additional compensation, impacting your effective hourly rate and cash flow.

Step 1: Build a Baseline Budget on Your Lowest Income Months

The first rule of managing fluctuating income is to base your lifestyle around your *lowest* predictable earnings, not your best months.

How to Calculate It:

- **Review the Past 12-24 Months:** Look at your total monthly income, identifying the months where you earned the least.
- **Identify the Bottom Line:** Find your "worst-case" month—or, better yet, average your three lowest months.
- **Set Your Baseline Budget:** Create a budget based on this lower figure.

This does two things:

- Prevents over-spending during high-income months.
- Creates a more resilient financial plan that can survive dry spells.

Your baseline budget should cover:

- Housing (rent or mortgage)
- Utilities
- Transportation
- Groceries
- Health insurance

- Debt payments
- Basic professional expenses (software subscriptions, licensure, continuing education)

Luxuries like vacations, shopping, and fine dining can be funded from income above your baseline, but should not be included in it.

Step 2: Build a "Feast and Famine" Fund

Think of this as an emergency fund—but tailored to the freelance or project-based lifestyle.

The Goal:

Save enough to cover 3–6 months of essential expenses.

But for freelance architects, a 6-month cushion is often more realistic given the length of payment cycles and the potential duration of slowdowns.

How to Fund It:

- Allocate a fixed percentage (say, 10–30%) of every invoice or project payment directly into your fund.
- Treat it as a non-negotiable operating expense—just like paying rent or utilities.
- During particularly busy periods, ramp up your contributions.

This fund acts as a buffer, smoothing out the dry spells and keeping your finances steady even when projects are sparse.

Step 3: Smooth Your Income with an Owner's Draw or Salary

One method that many solo practitioners and small firm owners use is paying themselves a steady "salary" from their business.

How It Works:

- Deposit all client payments into a business account.
- Pay yourself a fixed amount each month, just like a paycheck.

By controlling the outflow, you shield your personal finances from the ups and downs of project payments.

Benefits:

- Easier to budget personally.
- Reduces the emotional rollercoaster of fluctuating cash flow.
- Makes your taxes cleaner (especially if you've structured your business as an S-corp or LLC).

Step 4: Create a Tiered Budget Strategy

Income volatility requires flexible spending strategies. Here's a tiered model:

1. **Essentials Tier:** Mortgage, utilities, basic groceries, insurance.
2. **Lifestyle Tier:** Dining out, entertainment, modest travel.
3. **Luxury Tier:** Big vacations, tech upgrades, fine dining, discretionary shopping.

When cash flow is strong, you can fund all three tiers. During slower periods, you can scale back to essentials without panic.

Why This Works:

- Gives you flexibility to tighten or loosen your budget without emotional strain.
- Prevents guilt or regret during lean months.
- Helps protect your essential goals—like retirement savings—even when times are tough.

Step 5: Diversify Your Revenue Streams

Another key to managing unpredictable income is to not rely too heavily on one type of client or project.

Ideas for Architects:

- **Freelance Design Consulting:** Short-term, high-value gigs.
- **Teaching or Guest Lecturing:** Many architects supplement their income with adjunct teaching at local universities.
- **Writing or Speaking:** Publish articles, give talks, or conduct webinars.
- **Passive Income:** Create and sell architectural templates, online courses, or design kits.
- **Real Estate Investments:** Many architects successfully parlay their design expertise into smart real estate investments.

Diversifying income streams reduces reliance on one type of project or client and softens the impact of industry downturns.

Step 6: Understand Your Tax Obligations

Freelance and project-based income often comes without tax withholding, meaning you're responsible for your own quarterly estimated taxes.

Key Steps:

- **Set Aside Taxes Automatically:** 25–30% of every dollar earned should go into a separate tax savings account.
- **Understand Deductions:** Home office expenses, professional development, travel for client meetings, and software subscriptions can often be deducted.
- **Hire a CPA:** Particularly one who understands creative professionals or small business owners.

Taxes are not optional. Planning for them avoids the painful scramble every April.

Step 7: Rethink "Emergency Fund" vs. "Opportunity Fund"

While an emergency fund protects you, an opportunity fund positions you. An opportunity fund lets you:

- Invest in equipment upgrades.
- Fund a marketing campaign.
- Take on an exciting but underfunded project.
- Attend conferences or workshops that expand your network.

For architects, who often thrive on portfolio and reputation, having money set aside for strategic growth can be a career accelerator.

Step 8: Protect Your Business and Income

Beyond personal finances, protecting your business is key.

Essential Insurance Coverage:

- **Professional Liability Insurance:** Covers you if a client claims negligence or error.
- **General Business Insurance:** Protects against property damage or injury.
- **Disability Insurance:** Especially important for solo practitioners—what happens to your income if you're unable to work?
- **Health Insurance:** Non-negotiable, even if expensive.

Insurance isn't sexy. But it's an essential part of risk management when your income depends on your ability to work and deliver.

Step 9: Build Strong Contracts and Payment Terms

Contracts are your first line of defense against income instability.

Best Practices:

- **Clear Payment Schedules:** Include upfront deposits, progress payments, and final payment upon delivery.
- **Late Fees:** Discourage slow payments by including late fee clauses.
- **Change Orders:** Clearly define the process and cost implications if project scope changes.
- **Termination Clauses:** Protect yourself if a client relationship deteriorates.

Good contracts don't just protect you legally—they protect your cash flow.

Step 10: Master the Art of Client Communication

Finally, smooth cash flow often comes down to client relationships.

Best Practices:

- **Set Expectations Early:** Communicate payment terms at the outset.
- **Invoice Promptly:** Don't wait weeks to send invoices.
- **Follow Up Politely but Firmly:** A gentle nudge 5–7 days after the due date is appropriate.
- **Keep Clients Updated:** Frequent updates during a project foster goodwill and make clients more likely to pay on time.

Chapter 31: Tax Deductions and Credits for Architects

Financial literacy isn't just about growing your income—it's about protecting it. And one of the most underutilized tools architects have is the intelligent use of tax deductions and credits.

For many architects, taxes are an afterthought, often addressed once a year in a rushed meeting with an accountant. But proactive tax planning can substantially impact your financial stability and long-term wealth-building efforts. In this chapter, we will explore the unique deductions and credits available to architects, common pitfalls to avoid, and how to maximize legitimate write-offs without raising red flags with the IRS.

Think of this chapter as your blueprint for smarter tax management: a guide to architecting a financial life where more of what you earn stays with you.

Why Tax Literacy Matters for Architects

Architects, whether employed at a firm, running their own practice, freelancing, or consulting, have a financial landscape that is both complex and dynamic. With significant costs related to education, licensure, continuing education, software, travel, and client development, architects must be vigilant about every dollar.

Ignoring potential deductions doesn't just mean paying more in taxes—it means sacrificing money that could fund your retirement, invest in your firm's growth, or provide financial cushioning during industry slowdowns.

Moreover, architects who are self-employed or part of a partnership face a tax environment vastly different from their W-2-employed peers, making knowledge of deductions and credits not optional but essential.

Common Deductions for Architects

Let's start with a list of deductions every architect should know—and understand how to claim them properly.

Home Office Deduction

If you work from a dedicated space in your home, you may qualify for the home office deduction. This can be an incredibly valuable write-off if done correctly.

Key Rules:

- The space must be used **regularly and exclusively** for business.
- It must be your **principal place of business**, or where you meet clients.
- It doesn't have to be an entire room, but it must have clear boundaries (e.g., a designated area in a larger room).

Two Methods:

1. **Simplified Method**: $5 per square foot up to 300 square feet ($1,500 max).
2. **Actual Expense Method**: Deduct the proportionate share of actual home expenses—mortgage interest, rent, utilities, insurance, repairs.

Pro Tip: Document the size and use of your home office with photos and a floor plan sketch. Keep utility and repair receipts.

Software and Subscriptions

Modern architecture relies heavily on expensive software tools:

- CAD software (AutoCAD, Revit)
- Rendering software (Lumion, V-Ray)
- Project management platforms
- Cloud storage subscriptions
- Business software (QuickBooks, Adobe Creative Suite)

Deductible: The full cost of software subscriptions and updates if they are used for your work.

One-Time vs. Subscription:

- A one-time software purchase can be depreciated over its useful life (generally 3-5 years).
- Subscriptions are deducted in the year incurred.

Tip: Keep an organized list of software and renewal receipts.

Travel and Meals

Travel is common in architecture: site visits, client meetings, continuing education, conferences.

Deductible Travel Expenses:

- Airfare, hotel, rental cars
- 50% of meal costs
- Parking, tolls, taxis, rideshare
- Internet access fees at hotels

Conditions:

- Travel must be **primarily** for business.
- Maintain a log of trip purpose, locations, dates.

Meals:

- Must be directly related to business (client meetings, networking).

- Keep detailed receipts showing attendees and business purpose.

Licensing Fees and Professional Dues

Architecture is a licensed profession. License renewals, exam costs, and continuing education are necessary for practice—and are tax-deductible.

Examples:

- State licensure renewal fees
- NCARB membership fees
- AIA membership dues
- Continuing education courses
- Conference fees

Non-Deductible: Membership dues paid to organizations that are primarily for social purposes (e.g., private clubs).

Continuing Education and Certifications

To stay competitive, architects often pursue ongoing education:

- LEED accreditation
- Specialized certifications (WELL, Passive House)
- Professional workshops

Costs for these certifications, along with travel and materials, are generally deductible.

Bonus: If the course qualifies as improving your skills rather than teaching you a new profession, it's fully deductible.

Office Supplies and Equipment

From sketchbooks and pens to laptops and printers—if you purchase it for work, it's likely deductible.

Key Tips:

- Keep all receipts.
- For expensive items (computers, printers), you may need to capitalize

and depreciate or use **Section 179** to write off the full cost immediately.

Business Insurance

Insurance that protects your business is deductible:

- Professional liability (Errors and Omissions)
- General business insurance
- Health insurance (for self-employed architects)

Vehicle Use

If you use your car for business travel (not commuting), you can deduct mileage or actual expenses.

Two Methods:

1. **Standard Mileage**: IRS sets a per-mile rate (e.g., 65.5 cents/mile for 2023).
2. **Actual Expense**: Track gas, maintenance, insurance, and depreciate the car.

Rules:

- Keep a mileage log.
- Only business-related miles qualify (not commuting).

Tax Credits Relevant to Architects

Credits directly reduce your tax bill, dollar-for-dollar.

Energy Efficiency Credits

If you work on energy-efficient commercial building projects, you might qualify for credits under Section 179D.

Who Can Claim:

- Architects designing public buildings (schools, government).

- You must be certified as designing to specific energy reduction standards.

Research and Development (R&D) Tax Credit

Architectural firms engaging in innovation (energy efficiency, new construction methods) may qualify for the R&D tax credit.

Eligible Activities:

- Developing new construction techniques.
- Improving sustainability in design.
- Innovative use of materials.

Tip: Work with a CPA who specializes in R&D credits to properly document qualifying activities.

Lifetime Learning Credit

For architects going back to school for graduate degrees or additional certifications, tuition may qualify for this credit (up to $2,000 per year).

Audit-Proofing Your Deductions

Architects often operate in the "high audit risk" zones because of self-employment income and large deductions. Here's how to stay safe:

- **Keep Detailed Records**: Save receipts, bank statements, mileage logs.
- **Use Business Accounts**: Keep personal and business finances separate.
- **Avoid Red Flags**:
- Large home office deductions relative to income.
- Excessive meal and entertainment deductions.
- High vehicle expense claims without a mileage log.
- **Hire a Pro**: A CPA who understands architects can save you from costly mistakes.

Sample Tax Scenarios

Scenario 1: Solo Practitioner

Maria runs a one-woman architecture firm from a home office. She deducts:

- 200 sq ft of her home
- CAD and Revit subscriptions
- Travel to three client sites per month
- License renewal and AIA dues
- Laptop (Section 179 expensing)

She saves over $15,000 a year in taxes by documenting properly.

Scenario 2: Small Firm Partner

David, a partner in a 5-person firm, leverages:

- R&D tax credits for sustainability innovations.
- Section 179D for public school projects.
- Standard mileage for his business vehicle.

Careful planning saves the firm and partners thousands annually.

Scenario 3: Freelancer

Jen freelances on residential projects. She claims:

- Home office deduction
- Business insurance
- 50% of meals during networking events
- Courses for Passive House certification

She keeps digital receipts and mileage logs via an app.

Action Steps for Architects

1. **Set up a Bookkeeping System**: QuickBooks, FreshBooks, or a simple spreadsheet.
2. **Separate Business Accounts**: Use dedicated credit cards and bank accounts.
3. **Track Mileage**: Use apps like MileIQ or Everlance.
4. **Save Receipts**: Digitize them monthly.
5. **Hire a Tax Pro**: Ideally, one with creative professional clients.
6. **Review Deductions Quarterly**: Don't wait until April 14th.

Mindset Shifts

- **Think of Taxes as an Ongoing Project**: Like a long-term build, tax efficiency is year-round.
- **Respect Your Business**: Treat architecture like the business it is.
- **Invest in Professional Help**: Good accountants save you far more than they cost.

Conclusion

Architects are natural problem-solvers, adept at balancing creativity with constraints. Tax planning is just another project—requiring foresight, precision, and design thinking.

A strong tax strategy doesn't just save money. It frees up mental space, reduces stress, and supports the sustainability of your career.

And remember: the smartest architects don't just design beautiful buildings—they design sustainable financial lives.

Advanced Tax Strategies for Architects

Once you have the basic deductions under control, you can move into more advanced territory. These strategies won't apply to every architect at every stage, but understanding them will help you build a more sophisticated, resilient financial plan.

Section 179 Expensing and Bonus Depreciation

When you purchase significant business equipment—like computers, servers, furniture, or even vehicles—you can either depreciate the asset over several years or expense it upfront.

- **Section 179** allows you to deduct the entire cost of qualifying property in the year it's placed in service, up to a limit ($1.22 million for 2024).
- **Bonus Depreciation** allows for 60% immediate expensing of new (and used) business equipment purchases in 2024. This percentage is gradually phasing down after 2023 but still remains a powerful tool.

Use Case for Architects:

- Buying a new high-end laptop and large-scale printer for your firm.
- Investing in office fit-out if you move to a leased space (some improvements may qualify).

Tip: Consult a CPA before making large purchases—timing can affect your deduction eligibility.

Qualified Business Income (QBI) Deduction

The **QBI deduction** (Section 199A) allows eligible self-employed individuals and business owners to deduct up to 20% of their qualified business income.

Architectural firms are often eligible for this deduction, depending on total income and how the firm is structured.

Eligibility:

- For 2024, the deduction starts phasing out for single filers at $191,950 and married filing jointly at $383,900.
- Service-based businesses (like law firms and accounting firms) have more restrictions, but architects generally avoid these service-business limits.

Strategy:

- Maintain clear books to isolate business income from personal income.
- Be mindful of your taxable income to stay below phase-out thresholds.

Cost Segregation Studies

If you or your firm owns commercial real estate (e.g., your own office building), a **cost segregation study** can unlock significant tax savings.

What It Does:

- Reclassifies certain building components (lighting, HVAC, finishes) into shorter depreciation lives (5, 7, 15 years instead of 39).
- Front-loads deductions, improving cash flow.

Example:

- Without cost segregation: Straight-line depreciation of $1M building over 39 years = ~$25,641 per year.
- With cost segregation: Accelerated deductions can produce $100K+ in year-one deductions.

Solo 401(k) and Defined Benefit Plans

Self-employed architects and small firm owners can supercharge their retirement savings and lower taxable income:

- **Solo 401(k)**: As both employer and employee, you can contribute up to $69,000 in 2024 (plus $7,500 catch-up if 50+).

- **Defined Benefit Plans**: For high earners nearing retirement, a defined benefit (pension-style) plan can allow contributions of $100K-$250K+ annually.

Why It Matters:

- Huge deductions now.
- Tax-deferred growth.
- Powerful retirement savings vehicle.

Tip: Work with a retirement plan consultant or financial advisor to set up correctly.

Tax Pitfalls to Avoid

With opportunity comes responsibility. Certain missteps can trigger audits or negate potential savings.

Mixing Personal and Business Expenses

One of the fastest ways to get flagged by the IRS is to blur personal and business spending:

- Personal vacations disguised as "business travel."
- Non-deductible entertainment costs.
- Home office areas doubling as guest bedrooms.

Solution: Maintain strict boundaries. Only deduct what is legitimate, necessary, and documented.

Overstating Deductions

Claiming excessive deductions—especially for meals, home office, and vehicle mileage—can draw scrutiny.

Best Practices:

- Keep contemporaneous logs.

- Photograph receipts.
- Document client meetings and project site visits.

Ignoring Estimated Taxes

Self-employed architects must pay estimated quarterly taxes:

- April 15
- June 15
- September 15
- January 15 (of the following year)

Missing payments can trigger penalties and interest.

Tip: Use 110% of prior year's taxes as a safe harbor if your income is variable.

Misclassifying Employees

If you have staff, be clear on whether they are employees (W-2) or independent contractors (1099). Misclassification can lead to steep IRS penalties.

Building a Year-Round Tax Strategy

Rather than scrambling at tax time, successful architects integrate tax planning into their routine.

Quarterly Check-Ins

- Review income and expenses.
- Adjust estimated tax payments.
- Evaluate large upcoming purchases.
- Analyze profitability.

Annual Tax Planning Meeting

Meet with your CPA every fall (September-October) to:

- Project year-end income.
- Maximize retirement contributions.
- Plan purchases or deductions.
- Harvest tax losses on investments.

Automating Deductions and Documentation

Modern apps can make tax planning much easier:

- **MileIQ** for mileage.
- **Expensify** for receipts.
- **QuickBooks Online** for bookkeeping.

Architect-Specific Tax Insights

Architects and the R&D Tax Credit

Architects who focus on sustainable design, energy efficiency, or unique structural solutions often perform activities qualifying for R&D credits—even if they don't realize it.

Qualifying Examples:

- Developing new LEED-compliant building systems.
- Innovative use of environmentally friendly materials.
- Design of new prototypes for disaster-resilient structures.

Key: Keep documentation of project objectives, testing, and design challenges.

Energy-Efficient Commercial Buildings Deduction (Section 179D)

For architects who design government or public buildings, Section 179D can offer up to $5.00 per square foot (indexed for inflation) in deductions for energy-efficient systems.

Eligible Projects:

- K-12 schools

- Municipal buildings
- Libraries
- Public universities

Architects can claim the deduction if the building owner transfers the tax benefit to the designer (often done for public buildings).

Sample Tax Optimization Blueprint for an Architect

Profile: 45-year-old solo practitioner with a $300K income and a 2-person team.

Tax Strategy:

1. Home office deduction ($1,500 simplified method).
2. Vehicle mileage log (10,000 business miles = $6,550 deduction).
3. Software and subscription write-offs ($3,500).
4. Section 179 expensing for new computer equipment ($8,000).
5. SEP IRA contribution ($58,000).
6. 199A QBI deduction (20% of net business income = ~$48,000).
7. Quarterly estimated tax payments automated.
8. Evaluating 179D deductions on a public school project ($40,000).
9. Documenting sustainable design R&D activities for a $20,000 credit.

Result: Reduced taxable income by over $180,000, saving approximately $65,000 in taxes.

Action Plan: Architect Your Tax Strategy

1. **Hire a Specialist**: Find a CPA familiar with the architecture industry.
2. **Track Deductions Weekly**: Not quarterly—weekly.
3. **Plan Large Purchases Strategically**: Align with Section 179 or bonus depreciation benefits.
4. **Use a Mileage App**: Manual logs are outdated.

5. **Review Your QBI Status**: If your income is near the threshold, explore strategies to stay under.
6. **Claim Credits Aggressively (But Properly)**: Especially R&D and 179D.
7. **Build a Retirement Vehicle**: Maximize tax-deferred savings.
8. **Set Calendar Alerts for Estimated Taxes**: Avoid penalties.
9. **Automate Receipts**: Use technology to build a bulletproof audit defense.

Conclusion

For architects, taxes shouldn't be an afterthought, a burden, or an annual scramble. They should be a deliberate part of your professional practice—the same way you refine a design over iterative drafts.

Understanding the deductions and credits available to you, and using them wisely, allows you to keep more of your hard-earned income and reinvest it into what matters: your practice, your creativity, and your future.

The most successful architects don't just master design. They master their finances.

Because the smartest architects don't just design beautiful buildings—they design sustainable, prosperous lives.

Chapter 32: Sustainable Wealth Building for Architects

Introduction: The Blueprint for Wealth

Architects are uniquely trained to think long-term. They envision structures that endure for decades or even centuries. Yet when it comes to financial planning, even the most visionary architects sometimes fall into the trap of thinking short-term — paycheck to paycheck, project to project. This chapter is about shifting that perspective.

Just as a building needs a strong foundation, thoughtful design, and a plan for resilience, so does your financial life. Sustainable wealth building isn't about chasing the highest returns or risking everything for a big payoff. It's about the same principles you apply to architecture: design, structure, resilience, and timelessness.

In this chapter, we'll map out how to apply your skills as an architect to build a financial blueprint that can support you for life — and beyond.

Part 1: The Architect's Mindset for Wealth

Design Thinking Meets Financial Planning

Architects approach every project by defining the problem, understanding the client, studying the site, and creating thoughtful, elegant solutions. Financial planning, when done right, follows the same process:

- **Problem Definition**: What are your goals — financial freedom, security, legacy?
- **Site Analysis**: What is your current financial landscape — assets, liabilities, cash flow?
- **Schematic Design**: What investment and saving strategies align with your vision?
- **Construction Documents**: How do you implement systems and safeguards?
- **Resilience Planning**: How do you adapt your financial structure over time?

Your skills in balancing creativity and practicality are precisely what's needed to build wealth that is both functional and beautiful.

Embracing Delayed Gratification

Architecture teaches patience. The most iconic structures can take years to design and decades to complete. Wealth works the same way. Sustainable wealth is not about quick wins. It's built slowly through:

- Consistent saving and investing.
- Avoiding unnecessary risk.
- Letting time and compound interest do the heavy lifting.

Think of your wealth-building efforts as designing a cathedral, not a pop-up pavilion.

Risk Management: Designing for Resilience

A well-designed building anticipates stress — wind, earthquakes, heavy use. Similarly, a well-designed financial plan anticipates:

- Market downturns.
- Career disruptions.
- Health emergencies.

Resilience in finance means having:

- Emergency savings.
- Diversified investments.
- Insurance (life, disability, liability).

The goal is not to eliminate risk, but to design systems that can absorb shocks without collapse.

Part 2: Key Pillars of Sustainable Wealth Building

Pillar 1: Strong Foundations — Saving and Budgeting

Before you can build up, you must build solid foundations.

Emergency Fund

- 3 to 6 months of living expenses.
- Liquid, accessible — think high-yield savings accounts.

Budgeting for Stability

Budgeting doesn't have to feel restrictive. It's about allocating resources wisely, much like programming a building.

The 50/30/20 Rule:

- 50% Needs (housing, food, insurance).
- 30% Wants (travel, hobbies).
- 20% Savings and investments.

Architect Tip: Treat saving like a fixed expense in your life's budget, just like utilities or rent.

Pillar 2: Smart Debt Management

Architects often graduate with student loans, and many use financing for homes or businesses.

Good Debt:

- Invests in assets that appreciate (education, property, business equipment).

Bad Debt:

- High-interest consumer debt (credit cards, payday loans).

Tactics:

- Focus on paying off bad debt first.
- Consider refinancing student loans if interest rates are high.
- Use mortgages strategically — fixed rates, manageable terms.

Debt is a tool, like a beam or column. When used wisely, it supports growth. Misused, it collapses structures.

Pillar 3: Investment Strategy — Building Wealth Over Time

Investing is where sustainable wealth truly grows.

Asset Allocation

Like choosing materials for a building — steel, glass, wood — you choose a mix of:

- **Stocks** (growth)
- **Bonds** (stability)
- **Real Estate** (income and appreciation)
- **Alternative Assets** (private equity, REITs)

Diversification reduces risk and improves resilience.

Time Horizon

An architect designs differently for a temporary structure vs. a monument. Likewise:

- Short-Term (0–5 years): Keep assets liquid.
- Medium-Term (5–15 years): Balanced growth.
- Long-Term (15+ years): Embrace equities and compounding.

Pillar 4: Retirement Planning — Future-Proofing

Think of retirement planning as life-cycle costing for your financial life.

Essential Tools:

- 401(k)s and 403(b)s (for firm employees or academic architects).
- Solo 401(k)s or SEP IRAs (for independent practitioners).
- Roth IRAs and traditional IRAs.
- Health Savings Accounts (HSAs).

Maximize employer matches, contribute consistently, and let compounding work.

Catch-Up Contributions:

- After 50, you can save more into retirement accounts, accelerating wealth building as you near retirement.

Pillar 5: Protecting Wealth — Insurance and Legal Safeguards

Just like a building needs fire exits and structural reinforcements, your finances need protections:

- **Life Insurance**: For family and firm continuity.
- **Disability Insurance**: To protect your income if you can't work.
- **Liability Insurance**: Especially if you run a practice.
- **Estate Planning**: Wills, trusts, powers of attorney.

Future-proof your financial legacy the same way you ensure a building is safe and accessible.

Part 3: Lessons from Architecture Applied to Finance

Lesson 1: Design for Flexibility

Buildings must adapt to changing uses and needs. Financial plans must do the same.

- Regularly review and rebalance investments.
- Update your estate plan as family circumstances change.
- Stay agile in your career — new certifications, side businesses.

Lesson 2: Sustainability and Stewardship

In architecture, green design is about efficiency and long-term viability. In finance:

- Spend mindfully.
- Invest in companies and funds that align with your values (ESG investing).
- Focus on financial stewardship — it's not just what you earn, but how wisely you manage it.

Lesson 3: Form Follows Function

Good financial plans are elegant in their simplicity. Avoid:

- Overcomplicating investments.
- Chasing trendy assets.
- Over-leveraging with debt.

Simple, well-structured plans stand the test of time.

Lesson 4: Lifecycle Planning

Buildings have life cycles — conception, construction, maintenance, renovation, and eventual renewal or replacement. Your financial life follows a similar arc:

1. **Foundation**: Early career — saving, debt management.
2. **Framing**: Mid-career — wealth accumulation, career advancement.
3. **Finishes**: Peak earning years — optimizing taxes, estate planning.
4. **Maintenance**: Retirement — wealth preservation, income distribution.

Plan for each phase thoughtfully.

Lesson 5: Legacy Building

Great architects think about the future beyond themselves. Financially, legacy planning includes:

- Teaching your children or mentees about financial literacy.
- Structuring charitable giving.
- Leaving behind a sustainable practice or foundation.

Part 4: Practical Steps for Architects

Build Your Financial Blueprint

1. **Define Your Goals**: Retirement age, dream home, travel, firm ownership.
2. **Assess Current Position**: Net worth statement, cash flow analysis.
3. **Design Your Plan**: Budget, debt payoff, investment strategy.
4. **Implement Systems**: Automate savings, set recurring reviews.
5. **Monitor and Adjust**: Annual financial "site inspections."

Investing for Architects: Specific Considerations

- **Cyclical Income**: Use budgeting tools to smooth cash flow.
- **Project Bonuses**: Allocate windfalls to savings and investments.
- **Business Ownership**: Invest profits back into growth judiciously.
- **Continuing Education**: Budget for professional development — it's an investment in earning potential.

Mistakes to Avoid

- Delaying saving because of irregular income.
- Over-relying on the firm's success without personal diversification.
- Ignoring retirement accounts in early years.
- Underinsuring against life's unexpected events.

Inspirational Case Study: The Architect Who Built Financial Independence

Meet Elena, an architect who started with $80K in student loans. She applied disciplined savings, lived modestly, took on side consulting gigs, and maxed her retirement accounts. By 50, she had a portfolio worth $2 million and transitioned into teaching and small practice work — on her terms.

Conclusion: Designing a Life as Well as a Career

Sustainable wealth building is not a mystery. You already know how to do it — because you're an architect.

You design, plan, adapt, and build things that endure.

Apply those same principles to your finances:

- Lay the right foundation.
- Build with care and vision.
- Protect your creation against inevitable stressors.
- Adapt over time.
- Leave a legacy of beauty, strength, and purpose.

The smartest architects don't just design beautiful buildings—they design sustainable lives.

And they revisit their blueprints regularly, refining as necessary.

Your financial life deserves the same level of creativity, attention, and discipline as any building you'll ever create.

Chapter 33: Financial Literacy Checklist for Every Stage

Financial literacy is not a one-time class or a single chapter in your life. It's a living, evolving process, much like design itself. As an architect progresses through their career—from a wide-eyed intern to a seasoned principal—different financial milestones, risks, and opportunities arise. The blueprint you draft in your 20s won't serve you unchanged into your 50s or 60s. It must be revisited, renovated, and expanded.

In this chapter, we'll walk through the essential financial literacy checklist for every major stage of an architect's career. Think of it as your financial project lifecycle, with distinct phases, deliverables, and punch lists.

Senior Year of College: Laying the Foundation

Your last year in college is not just about completing your thesis or passing studio crits. It's also the best time to start laying the first bricks of your financial future.

Key Financial Goals

- **Create a Budget**: Track your expenses and understand where your money is going. Set up a basic spreadsheet or use apps to manage spending.
- **Build Credit Wisely**: If you don't already have a credit card, get a

starter card. Use it for small purchases and pay it off in full monthly.
- **Open a Checking and Savings Account**: If you haven't already, choose a bank or credit union with low fees and good digital tools.
- **Understand Student Loans**: Know how much you owe, your interest rates, and when repayments start. Explore grace periods and repayment options.
- **Set Up an Emergency Fund**: Even $500 can cushion you against unexpected expenses.
- **Learn About Retirement Accounts**: Familiarize yourself with 401(k)s, IRAs, and the magic of compound interest.

Action Steps

- Make a list of all debts—student loans, credit cards, any personal loans.
- Calculate your cost of living for six months after graduation.
- Start reading basic personal finance books or blogs.
- Look for internships or part-time gigs that offer stipends or school credit.

Mindset to Adopt

Think like a builder starting with the site plan. Before you lay the first beam, understand the landscape. In financial terms, that means learning the basics: budgeting, saving, debt management.

First Job: Framing the Structure

Your first professional paycheck feels momentous—and it is. But this is also where many young architects stumble financially, getting swept up in lifestyle inflation.

Key Financial Goals

- **Create a Post-Graduation Budget**: Now that you're earning, adjust your budget. Account for taxes, commuting costs, professional attire, and student loan repayments.

- **Employer Benefits**: Understand your firm's benefits—health insurance, 401(k) matching, commuter benefits.
- **Start Retirement Savings**: Contribute at least enough to your 401(k) to get the full employer match. More if you can.
- **Renter's Insurance**: If you're renting an apartment, get basic coverage.
- **Professional Licenses and Dues**: Budget for exam fees, licensure costs, AIA membership, or other professional groups.

Action Steps

- Set up automatic deposits: a portion into checking for expenses, a portion into savings for emergencies and short-term goals.
- Open a Roth IRA if you don't have a 401(k) yet.
- Pay more than the minimum on student loans if you can.
- Schedule annual financial checkups with yourself.

Mindset to Adopt

You're no longer just sketching—you're laying structural beams. It's time to set financial habits that can support more complex structures later. Good habits now will be load-bearing for decades to come.

Mid-Career: Building the Second Story

By now, you're an experienced architect juggling complex projects and possibly leadership roles. This is your prime earning phase—but also a phase where financial complexity increases.

Key Financial Goals

- **Increase Retirement Contributions**: Aim to contribute 15% or more of your income to retirement accounts.
- **Emergency Fund**: Expand it to cover 6–12 months of expenses.

- **Investment Portfolio**: Move beyond basic retirement accounts. Consider brokerage accounts, real estate, or other asset classes.
- **Family Planning**: College savings for kids (529 plans), life insurance, and updating wills or trusts.
- **Home Ownership**: If you haven't yet, this may be the time to buy a home. Consider proximity to work, resale value, and lifestyle needs.
- **Debt Reduction**: Aggressively pay down remaining student loans and high-interest debt.

Action Steps

- Meet with a financial advisor at least once every two years.
- Rebalance your investment portfolio annually.
- Set up automatic increases in your 401(k) contributions every year.
- Check credit reports annually for errors.
- Max out HSA contributions if available and invest the balance.

Mindset to Adopt

At mid-career, you're refining the design while ensuring structural integrity. It's about balancing growth with stability—pushing your income higher while protecting what you've built.

Pre-Retirement: Final Inspections and Punch List

You can see the finish line. Retirement is no longer abstract—it's a real, approaching event that needs careful preparation.

Key Financial Goals

- **Catch-Up Contributions**: Take advantage of IRS rules that allow higher contributions to 401(k)s and IRAs after age 50.
- **Maximize Social Security Strategy**: Plan carefully when to start claiming Social Security benefits.
- **Healthcare Planning**: Estimate healthcare costs in retirement, con-

sider long-term care insurance.

- **Downsize or Relocate**: If appropriate, sell the large family home and move to a more manageable, cost-effective space.
- **Estate Planning**: Finalize wills, trusts, power of attorney, and beneficiary designations.

Action Steps

- Calculate your expected retirement expenses in detail.
- Review your portfolio to reduce risk—move more into bonds or dividend-paying stocks.
- Review pension benefits or annuities if applicable.
- Consult with a CPA about tax-efficient withdrawal strategies.
- Make a list of post-retirement income streams—Social Security, pensions, rental properties, side work.

Mindset to Adopt

You are conducting a final walk-through before handing over the keys. Attention to detail is critical. Every crack in the foundation or poorly sealed window now could become a major problem later.

Universal Financial Principles

Regardless of stage, these core principles apply:

- **Pay Yourself First**: Always automate savings.
- **Live Below Your Means**: Lifestyle creep is the enemy of wealth.
- **Diversify**: Don't put all your financial eggs in one basket.
- **Plan for Taxes**: Understand how your choices affect your tax burden.
- **Protect What You Build**: Insurance, estate planning, and risk management are non-negotiable.
- **Stay Educated**: Financial markets, tax laws, and best practices change—stay current.

- **Update Your Plan Regularly**: Your blueprint isn't static. Review and revise it annually or after major life changes.

Common Mistakes at Each Stage

To build a resilient financial life, it's just as important to avoid the pitfalls as it is to follow best practices. Let's outline the typical mistakes architects make at different stages of their careers and how to steer clear of them.

Senior Year of College

- **Mistake: Ignoring Student Loan Terms**
- Many students accept loans without understanding the repayment schedules, interest rates, or deferment options. This can lead to nasty surprises after graduation.
- **Solution**: Educate yourself on loan types—federal vs. private, fixed vs. variable interest rates. Know your monthly payments before you graduate.
- **Mistake: Overborrowing**
- It's tempting to take out more than you need to enjoy a better lifestyle in college, but this debt will follow you.
- **Solution**: Borrow the minimum necessary and find side gigs to cover extra expenses.
- **Mistake: No Credit or Bad Credit Habits**
- Failing to build credit or misusing credit cards can damage your credit score early.
- **Solution**: Open a student credit card, charge small amounts, and pay it off every month.

First Job

- **Mistake: Living Paycheck to Paycheck**
- Many new graduates celebrate their new salary with higher rent, new cars, and expensive lifestyle choices without saving first.

- **Solution**: Follow the 50/30/20 rule: 50% needs, 30% wants, 20% savings.
- **Mistake: Skipping Retirement Contributions**
- Some new architects think retirement is too far off to worry about now.
- **Solution**: Start saving immediately, even if it's a small percentage. Early money has the longest time to grow.
- **Mistake: Not Understanding Benefits**
- Many ignore the fine print on healthcare plans, life insurance, and disability insurance.
- **Solution**: Attend HR onboarding sessions and ask questions. Understand what's offered and what you may need to supplement independently.

Mid-Career

- **Mistake: Lifestyle Creep**
- As salaries increase, many let their expenses balloon in proportion, leaving little for savings.
- **Solution**: Increase your savings rate with every raise before inflating your lifestyle.
- **Mistake: Neglecting Investment Diversification**
- Architects may pour everything into their 401(k) without exploring other investment vehicles.
- **Solution**: Diversify. Explore real estate, taxable brokerage accounts, HSAs, and other vehicles.
- **Mistake: Failing to Plan for Children's Education**
- College costs rise faster than inflation, and time flies.
- **Solution**: Open a 529 plan early and contribute regularly.

Pre-Retirement

- **Mistake: Underestimating Retirement Needs**

- Many miscalculate how much they'll need or overestimate Social Security benefits.
- **Solution**: Use conservative estimates. Plan for healthcare costs, inflation, and longer life expectancy.
- **Mistake: Holding Too Much in Stocks**
- Being too aggressive as retirement nears can lead to large portfolio losses.
- **Solution**: Shift to a more conservative, balanced portfolio five to ten years out.
- **Mistake: Ignoring Required Minimum Distributions (RMDs)**
- Penalties for missing RMDs from retirement accounts are steep.
- **Solution**: Know the age rules (currently 73 under SECURE 2.0 Act) and schedule automatic withdrawals if needed.

Sample Budgets and Financial Snapshots

Let's ground this with simple examples at each stage:

Senior Year of College: Monthly Budget

Category Amount

Rent/Utilities

$500

Groceries

$250

Transportation

$100

Cell Phone/Internet

$75

Health Insurance

Covered by parents/university

Entertainment

$100

Emergency Fund Saving

$50

Total

$1,075

First Job: Monthly Budget

Category Amount

Rent/Mortgage

$1,200

Utilities + Internet

$150

Groceries

$350

Transportation

$200

Health Insurance

$150

Retirement Contribution

$400

Student Loan Payment

$300

Entertainment

$150

Emergency Fund Saving

$200

Total

$3,100

Note: Allocate bonuses and raises strategically—50% toward savings, 30% toward debt reduction, 20% toward lifestyle upgrades.

Financial Timeline for Architects

This timeline shows key actions to take at different ages:

Age	**Milestone**
22	Graduate, start repaying loans, build emergency fund
23-25	Start 401(k), get renter's insurance, build good credit
26-30	Increase 401(k) contributions, pay off high-interest debt
30-35	Buy first home (if desired), start 529 plans
36-40	Diversify investments, revisit estate planning
41-50	Max out retirement accounts, reassess career trajectory
50-60	Catch-up contributions, reduce portfolio risk
60+	Finalize retirement budget, Social Security strategies

Case Studies: Real Financial Journeys

Case Study 1: Sarah, the Cautious Architect

Sarah started saving 10% of her income in her 20s, increasing by 1% each year. She bought a modest home in her early 30s and resisted upgrading to a larger one even as her salary increased. By 55, she had no mortgage, $1.5 million in her retirement accounts, and could afford to scale down to consulting work comfortably.

Lesson: Modest, consistent decisions compound over time.

Case Study 2: Mike, the Overextended Principal

Mike co-founded a firm but funneled too much into the business without saving personally. He bought a large home and expensive cars as his firm grew. When the 2008 recession hit, he had to lay off staff, sell the house at a loss, and delay retirement.

Lesson: Personal financial planning is as critical as business growth.

Architect-Specific Considerations

Architects have unique financial planning needs compared to other professions:

- **Licensure and Continuing Education**: Budget annually for maintaining licensure and professional development.
- **Client Payment Terms**: Expect long payment cycles; build reserves accordingly.
- **Professional Liability Insurance**: Essential for practice owners.
- **Economic Sensitivity**: Architecture is tied closely to real estate and public spending—be prepared for cyclical downturns.

Actionable Financial Checklists

Senior Year of College Checklist

- Understand student loan terms.
- Open checking and savings accounts.
- Establish initial budget.
- Apply for a secured or student credit card.
- Research 401(k)s and IRAs.
- Network for post-graduation jobs.

First Job Checklist

- Enroll in employer 401(k).
- Build 3-6 months emergency fund.

- Start student loan repayment aggressively.
- Get health, renter's, and disability insurance.
- Set up automatic saving for retirement and other goals.

Mid-Career Checklist

- Increase retirement savings to 15% of income.
- Diversify investments beyond retirement accounts.
- Review insurance policies.
- Set up college funds if applicable.
- Review and update estate documents.

Pre-Retirement Checklist

- Maximize catch-up contributions.
- Rebalance investment portfolio.
- Plan Social Security claim strategy.
- Review healthcare and long-term care needs.
- Finalize estate planning: wills, trusts, beneficiaries.

Mindset Lessons at Every Stage

Financial success is not just about technical knowledge—it's about mindset. Here are key mindsets for architects to adopt at every phase:

- **From Scarcity to Strategy**: Early-career architects often worry about money scarcity. Shift to a mindset of strategic growth.
- **From Expense to Investment**: See education, licensure, and even financial planning services as investments, not costs.
- **From Short-Term to Long-Term**: Think in terms of decades, not months.
- **From Solo to Collaborative**: Seek advice. Build a "board of directors" for your financial life: a CPA, a financial planner, a mentor.

- **From Passive to Proactive**: Your financial plan should not sit on a shelf. Review and refine it yearly.

Conclusion

Whether you are fresh out of school or preparing for a well-earned retirement, financial literacy is your most important tool outside the drafting board. It's not just about making money—it's about keeping it, growing it, and using it wisely to build a life that's structurally sound, resilient to shocks, and beautiful in its purpose.

Financial literacy isn't about denying yourself. It's about freedom—the freedom to take on the creative projects you want, to walk away from bad clients, to design without fear.

Because the smartest architects don't just design buildings—they design lives.

And just like every great structure, your financial life requires blueprints, load calculations, risk management, and, above all, thoughtful planning.

Remember: Review and revise your financial blueprint regularly, just as you would update a construction document set in a changing project environment. Your future self will thank you.

Chapter 34: Vetting Lawyers: The Questions You Must Ask

Lawyers are essential when you're dealing with contracts, liability, firm structures, intellectual property, and estate planning. Yet, many architects wait until there's a crisis to engage one—by then, it's often too late for proactive solutions.

Initial Questions

1. **Do You Have Experience Working With Architects or Creative Professionals?**

Architecture involves contracts, copyrights, intellectual property rights, and liability concerns specific to design work. You want someone who knows the industry.

2. **What Is Your Experience With Business Formation and Structuring?**

If you're launching a firm or restructuring an existing one, you need a lawyer who can advise on entity choice and draft partnership agreements, operating agreements, and shareholder contracts.

3. **Can You Help Me Protect My Intellectual Property?**

Your designs are your livelihood. A good lawyer will guide you on how to copyright plans, register trademarks (like firm logos), and protect other intellectual property assets.

4. **How Do You Bill for Your Services?**

- Hourly
- Flat-fee
- Retainer

Transparency is critical. Understand what you'll pay and how often.

5. **Do You Handle Employment Agreements and Independent Contractor Contracts?**

As your practice grows, you'll likely hire staff or subcontractors. You need proper agreements to minimize legal risks.

Deep-Dive Questions

6. **Can You Assist With Succession Planning or Practice Sales?**

If you're considering selling your firm or planning for retirement, your lawyer should understand buy-sell agreements, mergers, and acquisitions.

7. **How Will You Help Me Manage Professional Liability and Risk?**

They should advise on contracts that limit liability exposure, like limitation of liability clauses or indemnification provisions.

8. **What Is Your Approach to Resolving Disputes or Litigation?**

You want someone who will fight for you if necessary but also understands the value of mediation and settlement when appropriate.

9. **Will You Review Client Contracts and Consultant Agreements?**

A client contract that's poorly written can sink your business. Regular reviews ensure your agreements protect you as much as your client.

10. **How Do You Stay Current With Legal Issues Impacting Architects?**

Architecture law evolves—whether it's building codes, zoning changes, or professional liability standards. Your lawyer should stay informed.

Red Flags With Lawyers

- **No Industry Experience**: If they've never worked with architects, move on.
- **Vague About Fees**: Clear, upfront conversations about money are a must.
- **Poor Availability**: Your lawyer should be accessible when you need them, not three weeks later.

Comprehensive Checklist: Vetting Your Financial Team

Financial Advisors

Are you a fiduciary 100% of the time?

- How are you compensated?
- Do you have experience with small business owners, freelancers, and independent contractors?
- What is your investment philosophy?
- How will you help me manage irregular income?
- What retirement plans do you recommend for a solo architect or firm owner?
- How do you incorporate tax planning?
- Can you assist with other financial goals (college savings, real estate investment)?
- What happens if you leave or retire?

Will you collaborate with my CPA and attorney?

CPAs

- Do you work with independent contractors and small business owners?
- How do you stay current with tax law changes?
- Will you assist with tax planning, not just tax preparation?
- Can you help maximize deductions unique to architects?
- What strategies do you recommend for managing irregular income?
- Can you guide me on the best retirement plan for my business?
- Will you represent me in case of an IRS audit?
- How do you charge—hourly, flat rate, retainer?
- Will you collaborate with my financial advisor and attorney?

Lawyers

- Do you have experience working with architects and creative professionals?
- Can you help with intellectual property protection?
- What's your billing structure?
- Do you draft/review contracts and employment agreements?
- Can you assist with firm sales, mergers, or succession planning?
- What is your approach to dispute resolution?
- How do you stay current on architecture-related legal issues?
- Will you be available when I need timely advice?

Real-World Scenarios: Why Vetting Matters

Scenario 1: The Wrong Advisor

An architect hires a financial advisor without checking credentials. The advisor isn't a fiduciary and steers them into high-commission products that underperform. Years later, the architect realizes they've paid hidden fees and missed out on better growth.

Lesson: Vetting advisors protects your future wealth.

Scenario 2: Tax Disaster

An architect works with a CPA who isn't familiar with self-employed tax strategies. They overpay on taxes for years, missing out on deductions like home office, licensing fees, and software subscriptions.

Lesson: Specialized knowledge saves you money.

Scenario 3: Contract Chaos

A young architect signs a contract with a developer without legal review. The contract lacks proper indemnity clauses, and when a design flaw causes a costly delay, the architect is held fully liable.

Lesson: Good lawyers catch problems before they cost you.

How to Interview Financial Professionals

1. **Prepare Questions Ahead of Time**: Use the lists above.
2. **Treat It Like Hiring an Employee**: You're hiring for expertise and fit.
3. **Ask for References**: A good professional should have happy clients.
4. **Review Credentials**:

- CFP® for financial advisors
- CPA for accountants
- JD and specialization in small business or IP law for lawyers

1. **Trust Your Gut**: Professional fit matters.

How to Build Your Financial Advisory Team

- **Start Early**: Don't wait for a financial or legal crisis.
- **Think Long-Term**: You want people who will grow with your career.
- **Prioritize Communication**: Your advisors must be accessible and

proactive.

- **Integrate the Team**: Encourage collaboration among your financial advisor, CPA, and lawyer.

Action Steps

- Make a list of your current financial and legal professionals.
- Vet them using the questions and red flags above.
- Interview at least 2-3 new professionals if you don't currently have a solid team.
- Review your advisory team annually, just like you'd review a set of blueprints before construction begins.

Mindset Shifts for Architects

- **See Professional Advice as an Investment**: It's not a cost; it's a safeguard and a multiplier.
- **You Deserve Expert Help**: Your work is specialized and deserves specialized support.
- **Don't DIY Everything**: Architects thrive on collaboration; your financial life is no different.
- **Stay Informed**: Even with great advisors, maintain your financial literacy.

Conclusion

Architects spend years mastering their craft—why not apply the same rigor to building a financial foundation? By assembling a carefully vetted advisory team, you protect your creativity, your wealth, and your future.

Financial literacy isn't just about knowledge—it's about knowing who to trust. Just like you wouldn't pour a foundation without an engineer's input, you shouldn't plan your financial life without experts in your corner.

Remember: The smartest architects don't just design buildings—they design sustainable lives.

Review your advisory team regularly, ask hard questions, and never settle for less than excellence. After all, your life's design deserves it.

Chapter 35: Questions to Ask Financial Advisors, CPAs, and Lawyers

For architects, building a thriving financial life often requires a team of advisors. Much like you wouldn't design a building without consulting engineers or specialists, you shouldn't try to navigate the complexities of wealth, taxes, and legal planning alone. But how do you find the right professionals? More importantly, how do you vet them to ensure they understand the unique needs of architects—especially if you run your own practice or freelance?

This chapter will guide you through the critical questions you should ask financial advisors, certified public accountants (CPAs), and lawyers before hiring them. Think of it as due diligence—your blueprint for assembling a financial advisory team that's as solid as any structure you design.

We'll cover:

- How to vet a professional for architects' unique financial needs
- Key red flags to watch for
- What to expect from each type of professional
- Actionable steps to take before and after hiring

The Architect's Unique Financial Landscape

Before diving into the questions, it's important to recognize what makes an architect's financial situation different:

- **Irregular Income**: Many architects have project-based work, freelancing gigs, or firm ownership, making cash flow unpredictable.
- **Licensing and Continuing Education**: Ongoing costs for maintaining licenses and certifications.
- **Liability**: Architects face professional liability risks requiring specialized insurance and legal advice.
- **Economic Cycles**: Architecture is closely tied to real estate and construction, industries that are highly cyclical.
- **Long Career Horizons**: Many architects work well past traditional retirement ages, making long-term financial planning critical.

With these unique factors, it's clear why a generic, one-size-fits-all approach won't work.

Vetting Financial Advisors: The Questions You Must Ask

A financial advisor helps you manage investments, plan for retirement, and strategize for major life goals like buying property or starting a firm. But not all advisors are equal.

Initial Questions

1. **Are You a Fiduciary 100% of the Time?**
A fiduciary is legally obligated to act in your best interests. Not all advisors are fiduciaries. Some operate under a "suitability" standard, meaning they only have to recommend investments that are suitable—not necessarily best—for you.

- **Pro Tip**: Get their fiduciary status in writing.

2. **How Are You Paid?**

- **Fee-only**: Paid only by clients; no commissions.
- **Fee-based**: Fees + commissions.
- **Commission-only**: Paid by selling financial products.

For architects who value objectivity, a fee-only advisor is often best.

3. **Do You Have Experience Working With Small Business Owners or Independent Contractors?**

Freelance architects, solo practitioners, and firm owners have unique tax and retirement planning needs. An advisor unfamiliar with these structures may miss important strategies.

4. **What is Your Investment Philosophy?**

Some advisors favor aggressive growth; others prioritize capital preservation. Make sure their approach aligns with your goals and risk tolerance.

5. **How Do You Customize Financial Plans?**

Beware of cookie-cutter plans. Your financial plan should reflect your life, career stage, and goals.

Deep-Dive Questions

6. **How Will You Help Me Manage Irregular Income?**

Architects often experience feast-or-famine cash flow. A good advisor should help you set up systems to handle variability, like cash reserves or budgeting frameworks.

7. **What Retirement Plans Do You Recommend for Solo Practitioners?**

Expect them to discuss SEP IRAs, Solo 401(k)s, or SIMPLE IRAs, and why they recommend one over the other based on your income level and firm structure.

8. **Can You Assist With College Savings Plans (529s) or Other**

Specialized Accounts?

If you have kids, 529 plans can offer tax advantages for college savings.

9. **How Do You Incorporate Tax Planning Into Your Services?**

A great financial advisor should work alongside your CPA or offer integrated tax-efficient investment strategies.

10. **What Happens to My Plan If Something Happens to You?**

Ensure there's a continuity plan in place. You don't want your advisor to vanish without backup.

Red Flags With Financial Advisors

- **Pushing Products**: If they seem more interested in selling you insurance or annuities than building a plan, run.
- **Vague About Fees**: If they won't clearly explain how they get paid, it's a problem.
- **No Written Plan**: You should walk away with a written financial plan—no handshake deals.
- **High Client Load**: If an advisor manages too many clients, you may not get the attention you deserve.

Vetting CPAs: The Questions You Must Ask

A CPA isn't just for tax season. For architects, especially those with businesses, they are strategic allies.

Initial Questions

1. **Do You Have Experience With Independent Contractors and Small Businesses?**

Architects with S-corps, LLCs, or partnerships need tax strategies specific to business owners.

2. **Can You Help Me Set Up Retirement Plans for My Business?**

A good CPA can suggest plans that maximize retirement savings and minimize taxes.

3. **What Tax Strategies Do You Recommend for Managing Irregular Income?**

Look for strategies like income smoothing, estimated taxes, and deductions tailored to freelance or project-based income.

4. **How Will You Help Me Maximize Deductions?**

Expect advice on common write-offs like:

- Home office expenses
- Software subscriptions (AutoCAD, Revit, etc.)
- Licensing and continuing education fees
- Business travel
- Professional liability insurance

5. **What's Your Process for Handling IRS Audits?**

Make sure they will represent you and not abandon you if the IRS comes calling.

Deep-Dive Questions

6. **How Do You Stay Current on Tax Law Changes?**

Tax laws change frequently. You want a CPA who stays educated and proactive.

7. **Do You Offer Tax Planning, Not Just Preparation?**

Tax preparation is backward-looking. Planning is forward-looking and can save you thousands.

8. **Can You Help Me Plan for Large Expenses Like Office Renovations or Equipment Purchases?**

Architects often have significant write-offs related to setting up or expanding their firms.

9. **What Entity Structure Is Best for My Firm?**

They should be fluent in the pros and cons of sole proprietorships, LLCs, S-corps, and partnerships.

10. **Will You Coordinate With My Financial Advisor and Attorney?** True wealth management requires a team approach.

Red Flags With CPAs

- **Only Active During Tax Season**: You need year-round planning, not a once-a-year transaction.
- **Poor Communication**: If they don't respond to emails or calls promptly, that's a problem.
- **No Proactive Advice**: You shouldn't have to ask about deductions—you want a CPA who brings opportunities to you.

Chapter 36: Glossary of Financial Terms Every Architect Should Know

As architects, you speak the language of plans, elevations, and sections. In finance, a different language prevails — one that can seem just as foreign and complex if you haven't studied it carefully.

Mastering the fundamentals of financial terminology is critical to navigating personal wealth management, running a firm, planning for retirement, and protecting your future. This glossary is not exhaustive, but it focuses on the financial concepts and terms most relevant to architects at every career stage.

Treat this glossary the same way you treat your construction documents: as a reference set that grows with you, ensuring you make informed, confident financial decisions.

A

Adjusted Gross Income (AGI)

Your gross income minus certain deductions, such as student loan interest, retirement plan contributions, and health savings account contributions. AGI is important because it determines your eligibility for many tax deductions and credits.

Amortization

The process of paying off a loan in regular payments over time, where each payment covers both principal and interest. Understanding amortization is key when managing mortgages on personal homes, office spaces, or real estate investments.

Asset Allocation

The strategy of dividing your investment portfolio among different asset categories—such as stocks, bonds, and cash—based on your goals, risk tolerance, and investment horizon. A thoughtfully allocated portfolio can protect your wealth through market ups and downs.

Assets

Anything of value you own, including cash, investments, real estate, and even your architectural firm. Assets form the foundation of your net worth.

B

Balance Sheet

A snapshot of what you own (assets) and what you owe (liabilities) at a particular moment in time. Personal balance sheets are as essential as firm balance sheets for long-term financial health.

Basis Points (BPS)

One basis point equals one one-hundredth of a percent (0.01%). When negotiating investment fees or mortgage rates, small differences in basis points can add up significantly over time.

Beneficiary

The person or entity you designate to receive your assets—such as retirement accounts or life insurance—upon your death. Keeping beneficiary designations updated is crucial, especially after major life events like marriage, divorce, or firm ownership transitions.

Bond

A fixed-income investment representing a loan made by an investor to a borrower. Bonds are used by companies, municipalities, and governments to finance operations and projects. They tend to be less volatile than stocks but offer lower returns.

C

Capital Gains

The profit made from selling an asset, such as real estate or stocks, for more than you paid. Capital gains are taxable, and the tax rate depends on how long you held the asset.

Cash Flow

The net amount of cash moving into and out of your accounts. Positive cash flow is critical for the survival of both your household and your firm.

Certified Financial Planner (CFP)

A professional credential for financial advisors who have met rigorous education, examination, and ethical standards. Not all financial advisors are CFPs, so knowing this can guide you when hiring for your financial team.

Compound Interest

Interest earned on both the initial principal and the accumulated interest from previous periods. It's the cornerstone of long-term wealth building—think of it as financial gravity pulling your assets upward over time.

D

Deductible

The amount you must pay out-of-pocket before insurance covers expenses. This term applies to health insurance, liability insurance, and professional liability insurance (E&O) architects often carry.

Depreciation

The gradual reduction of the value of an asset over time. In a business context, architects can depreciate equipment, software, and even certain improvements to an office space, providing valuable tax deductions.

Diversification

A risk management strategy that involves mixing different investments within a portfolio. The goal is to minimize the impact of any one investment's performance on the overall portfolio.

Dividend

A distribution of a portion of a company's earnings to its shareholders. Some architects invest in dividend-paying stocks for regular income during retirement.

E

Emergency Fund

A reserve of cash set aside to cover unexpected expenses, such as medical emergencies or economic downturns. A rule of thumb is to save three to six months' worth of living expenses.

Equity

The value of ownership interest in an asset or business. For architects, equity might be in a personal home, an office building, or ownership stakes in their firm.

Estate Plan

A set of documents and legal strategies that dictate how your assets will be managed and distributed after death. Critical for architects with firm ownership, property holdings, or complex family situations.

F

Fiduciary

A person or organization legally obligated to act in your best interest. Always ensure your financial advisor is a fiduciary.

Fixed Expenses

Costs that remain constant month-to-month, such as rent or lease payments. Architects managing a firm must distinguish between fixed and variable expenses to maintain healthy cash flow.

Fiscal Year

A 12-month period used for accounting purposes that doesn't necessarily align with the calendar year. Some architecture firms operate on a fiscal year to match project cycles or tax strategies.

G

Grantor Trust

A trust where the grantor retains control and responsibility for taxes. Often used in estate planning to manage firm ownership succession.

Gross Income

Total income before taxes and deductions. This includes salary, investment returns, rental income, and business revenue for firm owners.

H

Health Savings Account (HSA)

A tax-advantaged savings account available to individuals with high-deductible health plans. Contributions are tax-deductible, growth is tax-free, and withdrawals for qualified expenses are tax-free—a triple tax advantage.

Home Office Deduction

A tax deduction available if you use part of your home regularly and exclusively for business purposes. Architects who freelance or run small firms from home should explore this benefit carefully.

I

Inflation

The general increase in prices over time, which erodes purchasing power. Inflation must be accounted for when setting long-term savings and retirement goals.

Individual Retirement Account (IRA)

A tax-advantaged investment account for retirement savings. Traditional IRAs offer tax-deferred growth, while Roth IRAs offer tax-free growth and withdrawals.

Index Fund

A type of mutual fund or exchange-traded fund (ETF) designed to follow a specific market index. Many financial advisors recommend low-cost index funds for long-term, passive investment strategies.

Intellectual Property (IP)

Creations of the mind such as designs, plans, and drawings that architects must protect legally through copyrights or patents.

J

Joint Tenancy

A form of property ownership where two or more people share equal ownership rights and the property passes automatically to the survivor(s) upon death. Architects married or partnered should consider the implications for real estate holdings.

K

Key Person Insurance

A life insurance policy on an individual critical to a business. For architecture firms, insuring a principal architect may protect the firm financially if that individual can no longer work.

K-1 (Form)

A tax document issued to partners in a partnership, showing income, losses, and dividends. Architects who are firm partners will need to become familiar with K-1s.

L

Liabilities

Financial obligations or debts. For architects, liabilities can include firm loans, mortgages, credit card debt, and unpaid taxes. Subtract liabilities from assets to calculate net worth.

Liquidity

The ease with which an asset can be converted into cash without losing value. Cash is the most liquid asset, while real estate is less liquid. Architects should maintain enough liquidity to handle firm expenses and personal emergencies.

Limited Liability Company (LLC)

A legal structure that protects personal assets from business debts and lawsuits. Many architects operate their firms as LLCs for the balance of liability protection and tax flexibility.

Line of Credit

A flexible loan from a bank that provides architects with access to funds up to a pre-set limit. Useful for managing cash flow fluctuations between projects.

M

Margin

Borrowing money to invest. While margin can magnify gains, it also magnifies losses. Most architects are better off avoiding margin in personal investments unless very experienced.

Market Capitalization

The total value of a company's outstanding shares. Larger market cap companies tend to be more stable, smaller ones can offer higher growth (and higher risk).

Medicare

Federal health insurance for people 65 and older. Architects planning retirement must understand Medicare's coverage and limitations, especially for long-term care.

Mutual Fund

An investment vehicle that pools money from many investors to purchase a diversified portfolio of stocks, bonds, or other securities. Mutual funds simplify diversification for individual investors.

N

Net Income

The amount left after subtracting taxes and expenses from gross income. For architects running a practice, net income determines how much they can pay themselves and reinvest in the firm.

Net Worth

Total assets minus total liabilities. Tracking your net worth over time is one of the best measures of financial progress.

Non-Qualified Retirement Plan

A retirement savings plan that doesn't meet the Employee Retirement Income Security Act (ERISA) requirements. Often used by high-earning architects for additional retirement savings beyond 401(k) limits.

O

Operating Expenses

The costs of running a business day-to-day, such as rent, salaries, and utilities. Managing operating expenses carefully ensures profitability for an architectural practice.

Opportunity Cost

The cost of forgoing the next best alternative when making a decision. Every dollar spent today is a dollar that can't be invested for tomorrow.

Out-of-Pocket Maximum

The most you have to pay for covered healthcare services in a policy period. After you spend this amount, your insurance pays 100% of covered services.

P

Passive Income

Earnings from rental property, limited partnerships, or other enterprises in which you're not actively involved. Many architects pursue passive income streams to supplement earnings and build wealth.

Portfolio

A collection of financial investments like stocks, bonds, real estate, and other assets. A well-constructed portfolio balances risk and reward.

Profit and Loss Statement (P&L)

A financial statement summarizing revenues, costs, and expenses over a period. For architecture firms, a P&L helps monitor financial health and guide decision-making.

Profit Sharing

A retirement plan that gives employees a share of a company's profits. Smaller architectural firms often use profit-sharing to attract and retain talent.

Q

Qualified Plan

A retirement plan that meets IRS requirements for tax benefits. Examples include 401(k)s and SEP IRAs, which offer tax advantages but have strict rules.

Qualified Business Income (QBI) Deduction

A tax deduction allowing certain business owners to deduct up to 20% of their qualified business income. Architects who are sole proprietors, partners, or S-corp shareholders may be eligible.

R

Required Minimum Distribution (RMD)

The minimum amount you must withdraw from retirement accounts annually, starting at age 73 (as of 2024). Failing to take RMDs results in steep penalties.

Return on Investment (ROI)

A measure of the gain or loss generated on an investment relative to the amount of money invested. Architects investing in equipment, software, or real estate should always calculate ROI.

Roth IRA

A retirement account where contributions are made with after-tax dollars but withdrawals in retirement are tax-free. A powerful tool for younger architects expecting higher future tax rates.

S

Self-Employment Tax

The tax paid by self-employed individuals to cover Social Security and Medicare. Architects running solo practices must budget for self-employment tax, which can be substantial.

Simplified Employee Pension (SEP) IRA

A retirement plan designed for self-employed people and small business owners. Contributions are tax-deductible, and plans are easy to set up and maintain.

Sole Proprietorship

A simple business structure where one individual owns and operates the business. Offers no liability protection, so architects often evolve to LLCs or corporations as they grow.

Subchapter S Corporation (S-Corp)

A legal structure that allows profits to be passed through to shareholders without corporate tax. Popular among architects for tax efficiency and liability protection.

T

Tax-Deferred

Earnings such as interest, dividends, or capital gains that accumulate tax-free until the investor withdraws them. Many retirement accounts offer tax deferral to promote long-term savings.

Term Life Insurance

Life insurance providing coverage for a specific period (e.g., 20 years).

More affordable than whole life and appropriate for architects looking to protect family or firm partners during their working years.

Trust

A fiduciary arrangement that allows a third party, or trustee, to hold assets on behalf of a beneficiary. Architects often use trusts for estate planning and business succession.

U

Umbrella Insurance

Liability insurance providing additional coverage beyond homeowners, auto, and even professional liability policies. It protects architects against lawsuits that could threaten personal assets.

Underwriting

The process by which insurers evaluate the risk of insuring a person or asset. Important for architects purchasing life insurance, disability insurance, or firm liability coverage.

V

Vesting

The process by which an employee earns non-forfeitable rights to employer-provided retirement plan contributions. Architects should understand vesting schedules when evaluating job offers.

Volatility

A statistical measure of the dispersion of returns for a given security or market index. High volatility investments can yield high returns but with greater risk.

W

Will

A legal document expressing a person's wishes for asset distribution after death. Every architect, especially those with firm ownership or intellectual property rights, should have an up-to-date will.

Working Capital

Current assets minus current liabilities. Indicates a firm's operational liquidity and efficiency.

X

Expense Ratio

A measure of what it costs an investment company to operate a mutual fund or ETF. Architects should be mindful of expense ratios, as lower ratios generally mean higher investor returns over time.

Y

Yield

The income return on an investment, typically expressed as an annual percentage. Architects investing for retirement should balance yield against risk and growth objectives.

Z

Zero-Coupon Bond

A bond that doesn't pay interest but is sold at a deep discount to its face value. It pays the full face value at maturity. Useful for architects seeking long-term, stable returns without annual income.

Why These Terms Matter for Architects

Architects manage complex systems daily, and personal and firm financials are no different. Understanding these terms empowers architects to:

- Build resilient financial structures.
- Make informed investment and tax decisions.
- Protect their business and family assets.
- Negotiate more confidently.
- Plan for a fulfilling retirement without fear or guesswork.

Chapter 37: Sample Budgets for Architects: Every Stage of Your Career

Financial literacy isn't just about knowing terms or memorizing rules — it's about applying principles in real life, in real time. Architects, like the buildings they design, go through different phases: starting out, growing into leadership, peaking in their practice, and eventually stepping into retirement. Each of these stages carries its own financial challenges and opportunities.

This chapter will walk you through sample budgets for each career phase:

- Entry-Level Architect
- Mid-Career Architect
- Late-Career Architect
- Retired Architect

Each budget is built around common income ranges, typical expenses, and savings targets for someone in architecture. These are templates — not rigid prescriptions. Use them as starting points to build your own financial blueprint.

The Entry-Level Architect

You're fresh out of school, or maybe you're a few years into your first real job. Your salary is modest, but your ambition is high. You're managing student loans, maybe living in a small apartment, and trying to balance saving with living.

Sample Income

- Salary Range: $55,000 to $75,000
- After-tax Monthly Income (estimate): $3,500 to $4,800

Sample Budget Breakdown

Housing (Rent + Utilities): 30%

Target: $1,050 to $1,400

Goal: Keep housing costs below one-third of your income. Consider roommates or a smaller space if needed.

Transportation: 10%

Target: $350 to $480

Public transportation, car payments, insurance, fuel. In large cities, a car may not be necessary.

Food: 10%

Target: $350 to $480

Groceries, occasional dining out. Learning to cook is a financial superpower at this stage.

Student Loan Payments: 10%

Target: $350 to $480

Standard repayment or income-based repayment depending on your total debt.

Insurance (Health, Renter's, Auto): 5%

Target: $175 to $240

Often subsidized by employer benefits; ensure you're covered adequately.

Retirement Savings (401k, Roth IRA): 10%

Target: $350 to $480

Enough to meet employer match if offered, plus any extra toward a Roth IRA.

Emergency Fund: 5%

Target: $175 to $240

Start building 3-6 months' worth of living expenses.

Personal/Entertainment: 10%

Target: $350 to $480

Gym memberships, Netflix, modest travel.

Professional Development: 5%

Target: $175 to $240

Licensure exams, continuing education, software subscriptions like SketchUp or Revit.

Miscellaneous: 5%

Target: $175 to $240

Cushion for unexpected expenses.

Key Financial Goals for Entry-Level

- Build a starter emergency fund ($1,000 minimum, growing to 3-6 months of expenses).
- Start repaying student loans aggressively if interest rates are high.
- Contribute enough to get full 401(k) employer match.
- Live below your means and avoid lifestyle creep.
- Invest in licensure and certifications that will increase your future earning potential.

The Mid-Career Architect

At 35-45, you're balancing more — maybe a mortgage, family, firm leadership roles, and heavier savings goals. Your income has grown, but so have the demands on it.

Sample Income

- Salary Range: $90,000 to $150,000
- After-tax Monthly Income (estimate): $5,500 to $9,000

Sample Budget Breakdown

Housing (Mortgage + Taxes + Insurance + Utilities): 25%

Target: $1,375 to $2,250

You may own a home now — keep total housing costs reasonable relative to income.

Transportation: 10%

Target: $550 to $900

Still modest — reliable but not flashy car, or public transit where available.

Food: 10%

Target: $550 to $900

Increased family size may push this higher, but cook at home where possible.

Student Loan Payments: 5%

Target: $275 to $450

Should be winding down loans or completely paid off by late 30s to early 40s.

Insurance (Health, Home, Auto, Life, Disability): 8%

Target: $440 to $720

Comprehensive coverage is key as responsibilities grow.

Retirement Savings: 15%

Target: $825 to $1,350

Maxing 401(k) contributions, adding IRAs or brokerage accounts.

Emergency Fund: 5%

Target: $275 to $450

Ensure 6 months of living expenses are accessible.

Education Fund (if kids): 5%

Target: $275 to $450

529 plan contributions for children's future college costs.

Personal/Entertainment: 10%

Target: $550 to $900

Family vacations, hobbies, entertainment — keep joy in the budget.

Professional Development: 2%

Target: $110 to $180

Continued investment in certifications, conferences, or professional organizations like AIA.

Miscellaneous: 5%

Target: $275 to $450

Cushion for surprises — home repairs, medical co-pays, etc.

Key Financial Goals for Mid-Career

- Aggressively save for retirement — aim for 2x to 4x your salary by age 40.
- Eliminate all consumer debt.
- Start college savings if you have children.
- Increase life and disability insurance coverage.
- Max out tax-advantaged retirement accounts.

The Late-Career Architect

At 50-65, you're peaking in your earning years. Retirement is on the horizon, and financial independence becomes the focus.

Sample Income

- Salary Range: $140,000 to $250,000+
- After-tax Monthly Income (estimate): $8,000 to $14,000

Sample Budget Breakdown

Housing (Mortgage or Paid Off + Utilities + Taxes): 20%

Target: $1,600 to $2,800

Mortgage may be paid off; focus on taxes, insurance, and maintenance.

Transportation: 8%

Target: $640 to $1,120

Reliable, low-maintenance vehicle — no need for extravagance.

Food: 8%

Target: $640 to $1,120

Family size may be shrinking; higher-quality food and dining experiences.

Insurance (Health, Long-Term Care, Auto, Umbrella): 10%

Target: $800 to $1,400

Long-term care insurance starts to make sense now.

Retirement Savings: 20%

Target: $1,600 to $2,800

Max out all retirement accounts — 401(k) catch-up contributions.

Emergency Fund: 5%

Target: $400 to $700

Ensure this is fully funded for peace of mind.

Personal/Entertainment/Travel: 12%

Target: $960 to $1,680

More frequent travel, hobbies, philanthropy.

Healthcare Costs: 7%

Target: $560 to $980

Save for out-of-pocket expenses and future medical needs.

Education Support (College for Children or Grandchildren): 3%

Target: $240 to $420

Helping with tuition or starting gifting strategies.

Professional Development/Consulting Income Transition: 2%

Target: $160 to $280

Prepare for part-time consulting or mentoring in retirement.

Miscellaneous: 5%
Target: $400 to $700
Catch-all buffer for surprises.

Key Financial Goals for Late-Career

- Eliminate remaining debt, including mortgages.
- Maximize catch-up contributions to retirement accounts.
- Finalize estate planning documents.
- Prepare a retirement withdrawal strategy.
- Consider downsizing or relocating for lifestyle optimization.

The Retired Architect

Now you're living off what you've built — the nest egg you designed carefully across decades.

Sample Income

- Retirement Portfolio Withdrawals + Social Security: $60,000 to $120,000 annually
- After-tax Monthly Income (estimate): $4,000 to $8,000

Sample Budget Breakdown

Housing (if downsized or mortgage-free): 20%
Target: $800 to $1,600
Preferably no mortgage — but taxes, insurance, maintenance remain.
Healthcare (Medicare, Supplemental Insurance, Out-of-Pocket): 20%
Target: $800 to $1,600
Biggest growing cost in retirement.
Transportation: 5%

Target: $200 to $400

Modest vehicle or ride-share services; less commuting.

Food: 10%

Target: $400 to $800

More time for home-cooked meals and health-conscious dining.

Insurance (Umbrella, Long-Term Care, Life if Needed): 5%

Target: $200 to $400

Ongoing coverage for protection.

Travel and Entertainment: 20%

Target: $800 to $1,600

Enjoy the freedom to travel more extensively.

Gifting/Charity: 5%

Target: $200 to $400

Planned charitable giving or family gifting.

Professional Involvement/Volunteer Work: 5%

Target: $200 to $400

Architecture judging panels, nonprofit board involvement.

Miscellaneous and Buffer: 10%

Target: $400 to $800

For unforeseen expenses — medical, home repair, inflation adjustments.

Key Financial Goals for Retirement

- Maintain sustainable withdrawal rates (typically 4% or less).
- Monitor and adjust portfolio risk to preserve capital.
- Keep healthcare costs under control.
- Enjoy the lifestyle you spent decades building — thoughtfully and confidently.

Chapter 38: Architecture Salary Benchmarks and Cost of Living Comparisons

When it comes to managing your career and personal finances as an architect, one of the most overlooked — but most powerful — tools is knowing where your dollars stretch furthest. Salary figures alone don't tell the full story. Cost of living can eat into even a six-figure paycheck, leaving you with less financial breathing room than you'd expect.

This chapter walks you through a practical, financial literacy–focused guide to architecture salary benchmarks and how to evaluate the true value of your paycheck based on cost of living in different cities.

We'll break it down into:

- Salary Benchmarks for Architects by Career Stage
- Understanding Cost of Living Adjustments
- Best Cities for Architects Based on Income and Cost of Living
- Real-World Scenarios to Help You Frame Your Choices
- Action Steps for Making Smart Career and Relocation Decisions

Salary Benchmarks for Architects

Salaries for architects vary widely depending on education, experience, firm size, specialization, and geographic location. Let's start by looking at a general range by career stage.

Entry-Level Architect (0–3 Years Experience)

Typical Titles: Junior Architect, Designer I

Annual Salary Range: $55,000 to $75,000

Entry-level architects can expect modest starting salaries, particularly in smaller firms or less expensive markets. Larger cities or high-end firms may offer more competitive pay, but often at the cost of a higher cost of living.

Mid-Level Architect (4–9 Years Experience)

Typical Titles: Project Architect, Designer II, BIM Specialist

Annual Salary Range: $75,000 to $105,000

With licensure and a few years under your belt, you start seeing a tangible jump in earnings. Mid-career architects who have specialized skills — in sustainability, healthcare design, or commercial projects, for example — may command salaries toward the higher end of this range.

Senior Architect (10–20+ Years Experience)

Typical Titles: Senior Architect, Project Manager, Studio Lead

Annual Salary Range: $100,000 to $160,000

Senior architects overseeing projects or teams can command significantly higher salaries. Larger firms, especially those doing international work or major civic projects, tend to pay at the top end.

Principal/Partner Level (20+ Years, Ownership Stake)

Typical Titles: Principal, Partner, Managing Director

Annual Salary Range: $140,000 to $300,000+

At the ownership level, salaries are typically supplemented by profit-sharing or equity stakes in the firm. Earnings can vary dramatically based on firm success and personal book of business.

Understanding Cost of Living Adjustments

High salaries in major cities can be misleading. An $80,000 salary in New York City doesn't stretch nearly as far as $80,000 in a smaller city like Raleigh or Austin.

Key Factors in Cost of Living:

- Housing (rent, home prices, property taxes)
- Utilities and Energy Costs
- Transportation (public transit, car ownership)
- Healthcare
- Food and Groceries
- State and Local Taxes
- Insurance Costs

Cost of living is often expressed as an index. The national average is set at 100. A city with a cost of living index of 120 is 20% more expensive than the average; 80 is 20% less expensive.

Understanding how salary and cost of living interact is critical to making informed career decisions.

Best Cities for Architects Based on Income and Cost of Living

Let's look at cities where architects can build both rewarding careers and sound financial futures.

Best High-Salary, Moderate-Cost Cities

These cities offer strong salaries relative to their cost of living:

1. Dallas, Texas

- Average Architect Salary: $90,000
- Cost of Living Index: 92

2. Minneapolis, Minnesota

- Average Architect Salary: $88,000
- Cost of Living Index: 98

3. Raleigh, North Carolina

- Average Architect Salary: $85,000
- Cost of Living Index: 94

4. Atlanta, Georgia

- Average Architect Salary: $87,000
- Cost of Living Index: 95

5. Denver, Colorado

- Average Architect Salary: $92,000
- Cost of Living Index: 110
- Note: Denver's cost of living has risen sharply, but salaries have kept

pace.

Best Cities for Career Growth and Long-Term Financial Gain

High demand for architects often translates into job security and upward mobility:

1. Austin, Texas

- Booming tech and residential sectors.

2. Nashville, Tennessee

- Rapid growth in healthcare and commercial architecture.

3. Charlotte, North Carolina

- Financial sector growth driving commercial architecture demand.

Challenging Cities: High Salary, High Cost of Living

These cities offer high salaries — but also high living costs:

1. San Francisco, California

- Average Architect Salary: $105,000
- Cost of Living Index: 244

2. New York City, New York

- Average Architect Salary: $100,000
- Cost of Living Index: 187

3. Boston, Massachusetts

- Average Architect Salary: $98,000
- Cost of Living Index: 163

While these cities offer unparalleled professional exposure, the financial strain can be considerable unless salaries are well above average.

Affordable Cities for Architects

Lower living costs mean you can save more, even if the salary is slightly lower:

1. Kansas City, Missouri

- Average Architect Salary: $78,000
- Cost of Living Index: 85

2. Indianapolis, Indiana

- Average Architect Salary: $76,000
- Cost of Living Index: 82

3. Pittsburgh, Pennsylvania

- Average Architect Salary: $80,000
- Cost of Living Index: 87

4. Oklahoma City, Oklahoma

- Average Architect Salary: $74,000
- Cost of Living Index: 80

These markets are often overlooked, but they can offer an excellent quality of life and more disposable income.

Real-World Scenarios for Architects

Scenario 1:

You're offered a $100,000 job in San Francisco and an $80,000 job in Raleigh.

After factoring cost of living, your Raleigh salary offers better purchasing power — and a higher quality of life.

Scenario 2:

You're an entry-level architect trying to decide between living in Austin ($70,000 salary, rising costs) or Kansas City ($60,000 salary, low cost of living).

The extra $10,000 in Austin may be eaten by rent and taxes, while in Kansas City, you can build savings faster.

Action Steps for Smart Career and Relocation Decisions

1. Research Salaries Carefully

Use resources like the AIA Compensation Report, Glassdoor, and industry surveys.

2. Adjust for Cost of Living

Use online calculators to adjust salaries for different cities. Don't just look at gross numbers.

3. Consider Taxes

State and local taxes can make a big difference. States like Texas and Florida have no state income tax.

4. Think Long-Term

Will this city offer not just a job, but a sustainable career and lifestyle?

5. Visit Before You Leap

If possible, spend time in a prospective city before relocating. Neighborhoods, commute times, and local culture matter.

6. Budget Accordingly

Higher-cost cities may require more roommates, smaller spaces, or tighter budgeting early on.

Sample Monthly Take-Home Pay Comparisons

Let's move beyond gross salary to what really matters: how much you get to keep and spend each month after taxes and deductions.

For simplicity, assume:

- Single filer
- Standard deduction
- No dependents
- Pre-tax retirement contributions of 10% to a 401(k)
- Standard federal and applicable state taxes

San Francisco, California

Gross Annual Salary: $105,000

Federal + State Taxes + FICA: ~$31,000

401(k) Contribution (10%): $10,500

Net Income: ~$63,500

Monthly Take-Home: ~$5,290

Average Rent for One-Bedroom: ~$3,000

Remaining Monthly Budget: ~$2,290

Raleigh, North Carolina

Gross Annual Salary: $85,000

Federal + State Taxes + FICA: ~$22,500

401(k) Contribution (10%): $8,500

Net Income: ~$54,000

Monthly Take-Home: ~$4,500

Average Rent for One-Bedroom: ~$1,400

Remaining Monthly Budget: ~$3,100

Kansas City, Missouri

Gross Annual Salary: $78,000

Federal + State Taxes + FICA: ~$19,500

401(k) Contribution (10%): $7,800

Net Income: ~$50,700

Monthly Take-Home: ~$4,225
Average Rent for One-Bedroom: ~$1,050
Remaining Monthly Budget: ~$3,175

Boston, Massachusetts

Gross Annual Salary: $98,000
Federal + State Taxes + FICA: ~$27,500
401(k) Contribution (10%): $9,800
Net Income: ~$60,700
Monthly Take-Home: ~$5,058
Average Rent for One-Bedroom: ~$2,700
Remaining Monthly Budget: ~$2,358

Austin, Texas

Gross Annual Salary: $92,000
Federal Taxes + FICA (no state tax): ~$21,000
401(k) Contribution (10%): $9,200
Net Income: ~$61,800
Monthly Take-Home: ~$5,150
Average Rent for One-Bedroom: ~$1,700
Remaining Monthly Budget: ~$3,450

Housing Affordability Case Studies

Housing costs are the most significant part of most architects' budgets. Let's look at how much home you could reasonably afford in different cities, based on the classic guideline that your mortgage should not exceed 28% of your gross income.

San Francisco

Salary: $105,000
Affordable Monthly Housing Payment (28%): ~$2,450

Reality: The median home price exceeds $1,300,000, requiring a much larger income or a hefty down payment.

Raleigh

Salary: $85,000

Affordable Monthly Housing Payment (28%): ~$1,985

Reality: Median home prices hover around $420,000. Much more attainable for a mid-career architect.

Kansas City

Salary: $78,000

Affordable Monthly Housing Payment (28%): ~$1,820

Reality: Median home prices are around $290,000, making homeownership highly feasible even early in your career.

Boston

Salary: $98,000

Affordable Monthly Housing Payment (28%): ~$2,280

Reality: Median home prices are over $650,000, challenging but possible with dual incomes or larger down payments.

Austin

Salary: $92,000

Affordable Monthly Housing Payment (28%): ~$2,145

Reality: Median home prices around $460,000; competitive, but achievable depending on the neighborhood.

Detailed Strategies for Negotiating Salary Adjustments

Salary negotiation isn't just for new jobs. Architects at any stage of their career can and should revisit compensation based on cost of living, firm performance, and personal value added.

When to Negotiate

- Upon receiving a job offer
- During annual reviews
- After completing a major project successfully
- When market conditions shift dramatically (cost of living spike, new licensure, or specialized certification)

How to Prepare

- Research salary benchmarks for your city, firm size, and specialty.
- Prepare a "value document" outlining recent contributions: projects delivered, clients retained, new business generated.
- Know the cost of living increases in your area—especially if you live in a rapidly inflating market.

Common Mistakes to Avoid

- Negotiating without data.
- Accepting the first offer without countering.
- Focusing solely on salary—also consider benefits, bonuses, flex time, remote work, and professional development budgets.

What to Ask For

- Base salary increase
- Signing or performance bonus
- Increased firm contribution to retirement plans
- Funding for additional licensure or certifications
- Relocation stipends if moving to a high-cost city

Best Cities for Specific Architect Specialties

Different cities cater to different types of architects.

Healthcare Architects

Top Cities: Houston, Boston, Minneapolis

Why: Strong healthcare infrastructure and institutional investment.

Sustainable Design Experts

Top Cities: Portland, San Francisco, Seattle

Why: High demand for LEED certification and green building initiatives.

Residential Architects

Top Cities: Charlotte, Raleigh, Dallas

Why: Rapid residential growth and suburban expansion.

Commercial Architects

Top Cities: New York, Chicago, Los Angeles

Why: Concentration of corporate HQs and real estate development.

Hidden Factors Beyond Salary and Cost of Living

Remember to factor in:

- Commute times
- Quality of public transit
- Access to clients and projects you're passionate about
- Cultural amenities (museums, libraries, design scenes)
- Professional networking opportunities
- State licensure reciprocity — important if you move often
- Natural disasters or climate risk (wildfires, hurricanes, flooding)
- Long-term housing price appreciation — can affect net worth growth

Example Architect Lifestyle Budgets By City

Let's apply real numbers to lifestyle budgets for an architect making $90,000 in three different cities.

San Francisco

- Rent: $3,200
- Utilities: $200
- Transportation (public + occasional car share): $250
- Food: $600
- Entertainment and dining: $500
- Savings: $1,000
- Retirement contributions (pre-tax): $9,000/year
- Net discretionary income: Limited

Raleigh

- Rent: $1,400
- Utilities: $150
- Transportation (car ownership): $400
- Food: $500
- Entertainment and dining: $400
- Savings: $1,500
- Retirement contributions (pre-tax): $9,000/year
- Net discretionary income: Healthy

Kansas City

- Rent: $1,000
- Utilities: $150
- Transportation (car ownership): $300
- Food: $400
- Entertainment and dining: $350
- Savings: $2,000
- Retirement contributions (pre-tax): $9,000/year
- Net discretionary income: Strong surplus

Final Thoughts: Architect Your Career with Intent

Choosing where to live and work isn't just a lifestyle decision—it's a financial one.

- A flashy salary in a high-cost city may look great on paper but yield little real wealth building.
- A lower-cost city with moderate salaries might allow for earlier homeownership, higher savings rates, and a better work-life balance.
- Personal and professional goals should be balanced: consider whether being in a big design firm in NYC matters more to you than owning a

home sooner in a smaller city.

Financial literacy isn't just about budgets or investments—it's about being intentional with every decision. As an architect, you have an advantage: you already think in systems, scales, and long-term outcomes. Apply that same thinking to your financial life.

The smartest architects don't just design beautiful buildings—they design sustainable careers, meaningful lifestyles, and resilient financial futures.

Chapter 39: Red Flags to Watch For: Financial Scams and Schemes Targeting Creative Professionals

One of the most overlooked risks for architects—and for many creative professionals—is the unique vulnerability they face to financial scams and schemes. As a profession built on creativity, vision, and trust, architects are often wired to focus on the future, on design problems, on what could be—not always on what could go wrong. And scammers know that. They know creative professionals, especially independent architects, freelancers, and small firm owners, can sometimes be so focused on craft that they leave gaps in their financial defenses.

In this chapter, we'll talk about the red flags you need to recognize early—and strategies you can use to protect yourself and your practice.

Because designing your financial life isn't just about growth—it's about protection.

Why Are Creative Professionals Targeted?

Before we dive into specific schemes, it's important to understand why architects and other creatives are so frequently targeted.

- Many architects operate as solo practitioners or in small firms, without the institutional protections that larger businesses have.
- Creative professionals often work project to project, which can create

financial anxiety and vulnerability to "too good to be true" offers.
- Trust is foundational to how architects work—with clients, consultants, and communities—which scammers can exploit.
- Many creatives don't prioritize financial literacy early in their careers, making them easier marks for complex-sounding cons.
- The rise of digital platforms has made it easier for bad actors to target professionals across the country, even internationally.

Understanding these vulnerabilities doesn't make you weak—it makes you smarter. Let's talk about the specific schemes you need to watch out for.

Common Financial Scams Targeting Architects

Advance Fee Scams

How It Works:

You're approached—usually via email or through a professional platform—with an offer to participate in a lucrative design competition, high-profile project, or publication. The catch? You need to pay a registration fee, handling fee, or processing fee upfront.

Red Flags:

- Vague project details or competition rules.
- Poor grammar or unprofessional communication.
- Requests for wire transfers or payment via gift cards.
- Pressure to act quickly or lose your "exclusive opportunity."

Defense:

- Research the organization or event independently.
- Never pay an upfront fee for work or exposure.
- Validate through professional networks or trusted industry associations.

Phony Client Overpayment

How It Works:

A "client" contacts you with a small project or consultation. They send a check for more than the agreed amount and request you send back the difference. Days later, the check bounces, and you're out the funds you sent.

Red Flags:

- A check larger than agreed upon, with a polite but urgent request for refunding the balance.
- Vague project descriptions.
- Unverifiable contact information.
- Requests to communicate only via text or unofficial email accounts.

Defense:

- Never refund an overpayment—insist on reissuing a correct payment.
- Wait for checks to clear fully (even if the bank shows a temporary deposit).
- Work through established contracts and verified payment platforms.

Investment Schemes

How It Works:

You're approached by someone offering a "guaranteed" return on an investment in real estate, crypto, or a "new financial model" specifically tailored for creative professionals.

Red Flags:

- "Guaranteed" returns (legitimate investments always involve risk).
- Pressure to commit quickly, often tied to limited-time offers.
- Lack of clear documentation or prospectus.

- Promises of outsized returns compared to industry norms.

Defense:

- Never invest without independent verification.
- Consult with a fiduciary financial advisor before committing funds.
- Remember: If it sounds too good to be true, it probably is.

Phishing and Identity Theft

How It Works:

You receive an email appearing to be from a trusted source—your bank, a client, or a professional platform—requesting you to verify sensitive information.

Red Flags:

- Unsolicited requests for login credentials, social security numbers, or bank details.
- Slight misspellings in email addresses (e.g., ".co" instead of ".com").
- Urgent language that plays on fear ("Your account will be suspended unless you act now!").

Defense:

- Never click on email links from unverified sources.
- Always access sensitive accounts directly from the official website.
- Enable two-factor authentication whenever possible.

Fake Awards and Recognition Schemes

How It Works:

You receive notification that you've won an award—but you have to pay to receive it or be featured.

Red Flags:

- Awards you didn't apply for.
- Requirements to pay for plaques, certificates, or "mandatory" magazine features.
- Grandiose titles from unknown organizations.

Defense:

- Legitimate awards never require payment to accept recognition.
- Research the organization offering the award.
- Consult peers or professional organizations about legitimacy.

Invoice Fraud

How It Works:

Scammers pose as a trusted vendor or consultant and submit fake invoices, banking on you being too busy to notice.

Red Flags:

- Unfamiliar account numbers or bank details.
- Invoices that don't match contract terms or previously agreed amounts.
- Changes in payment instructions without official notice.

Defense:

- Implement strict invoice approval processes.
- Confirm changes in payment instructions via phone calls to trusted contacts.
- Use secure, professional accounting software with built-in protections.

Broader Schemes to Watch: Lifestyle Creep and "Success Traps"

Not all financial traps are obvious scams—some are hidden in the architecture of professional success itself.

Lifestyle Creep

How It Works:

As your income rises, so do your expenses, often unconsciously. A nicer car, a bigger house, more expensive vacations—until your rising income no longer creates more financial security.

Red Flags:

- You're making more money but still feel financially stressed.
- Increases in discretionary spending outpace increases in savings or investments.
- You find yourself "needing" things that were once luxuries.

Defense:

- Automate savings and retirement contributions to grow with income.
- Conduct annual financial reviews to align spending with goals.
- Remember: Lifestyle is a choice; security is the foundation.

Predatory Business Coaching or Mastermind Groups

How It Works:

You're promised elite access to a "mastermind" group or one-on-one business coaching for architects—but at exorbitant costs.

Red Flags:

- Lack of clear deliverables.

- Testimonials that seem too uniform or scripted.
- High-pressure sales tactics ("This offer closes tonight!").

Defense:

- Verify credentials and client outcomes independently.
- Be wary of non-refundable deposits or contracts without exit clauses.
- Invest cautiously and incrementally in professional development.

Action Steps to Safeguard Yourself and Your Firm

Due Diligence Checklist

- Verify identities and credentials.
- Ask for documentation.
- Research third-party reviews (not just testimonials).
- Consult with trusted peers or mentors before major financial decisions.
- Trust your instincts: If something feels off, investigate further.

Ongoing Practices

- Maintain up-to-date cybersecurity measures.
- Secure sensitive documents and back them up regularly.
- Use two-factor authentication for important accounts.
- Separate personal and business finances to reduce exposure.
- Have professional liability insurance to guard against legal exposure.

Real-World Scenarios: How Architects Have Been Targeted

The Vanity Publication Trap

An emerging architect received an email inviting them to be featured in a prestigious-looking design magazine—for a fee of $2,500. After paying, they never saw the feature or the magazine in circulation.

The Client Overpayment Con

A freelancer accepted a residential remodel project and received a check for double the agreed fee. They refunded the excess—only to find the original check was fraudulent.

The Cryptocurrency Investment Scam

A mid-career architect was invited by a "financial advisor" to invest in a crypto platform promising 30% annual returns. They invested a significant sum, only to lose all of it within months when the platform disappeared.

Empowerment Through Vigilance

Financial freedom isn't just about earning more—it's about protecting what you have. Scams evolve constantly, but vigilance, skepticism, and structured decision-making can dramatically lower your risk.

Remember:

- **Pause** before making financial decisions under pressure.
- **Verify** every financial relationship, especially new ones.
- **Consult** trusted advisors who have your best interests at heart.

You already have the skills as an architect—diligence, attention to detail, systems thinking. Apply them to your financial decisions, and you'll build a career and life that are both creatively fulfilling and financially secure.

The smartest architects don't just design beautiful buildings—they design safe, resilient financial foundations.

Chapter 40: Architect's Annual Financial Review Template

Why Architects Need an Annual Financial Review

As an architect, you wouldn't deliver a project without a final review—a closeout punch list, a set of as-builts, a post-mortem discussion with the team. You understand the value of reflection, iteration, and continuous improvement.

Your financial life is no different. An annual financial review serves as your personal post-occupancy evaluation of the structures you've built in your finances over the year. It's the process of taking a step back from the projects, the deadlines, and the design work to evaluate whether your financial systems are functioning as intended—and where they need recalibration.

Skipping this review is like skipping the final inspection of a building. The risk of cracks, leaks, and structural failures increases. Over time, small issues left unchecked turn into big problems. But with an annual financial review, you have the chance to course-correct, optimize, and build on your past successes.

This chapter provides a full blueprint for conducting your own financial post-mortem—a structured, repeatable process you can return to every year, much like an architect returning to a trusted set of standards.

Overview of the Annual Financial Review Process

The financial review process is built on six main pillars:

1. Income Review
2. Expense Audit
3. Savings and Investment Check
4. Debt and Liability Review
5. Insurance and Risk Management Review
6. Goal Alignment and Future Planning

Let's walk through each one carefully and systematically, just like you would with a set of construction documents.

Step 1: Income Review

Gather Your Data

Start with the basics: What did you earn this year? This includes:

- Salary or wages
- Bonuses or commissions
- Freelance or consulting income
- Rental property income (if applicable)
- Dividend and interest income
- Royalties or other intellectual property income
- Any side business revenue

Pull copies of your pay stubs, 1099s, bank statements, brokerage statements, and invoices to ensure nothing is missed.

Questions to Ask

- Did your income grow, stay flat, or decline compared to last year?
- Is your income diversified, or are you heavily dependent on one source?
- Are there predictable ebbs and flows, or does your cash flow feel unstable?

Action Items

- Identify opportunities to diversify your income.
- Consider adding a secondary income stream—consulting, teaching, product design.
- Adjust your estimated tax payments or withholding if your income structure changed.

Step 2: Expense Audit

Gather Your Data

Print out 12 months of credit card statements, bank statements, and any software-based expense tracking reports you have (e.g., from QuickBooks, Mint, or YNAB).

Categorize expenses into:

- Essential living expenses (housing, utilities, groceries)
- Business expenses (software, subscriptions, travel)
- Professional development (conferences, courses)
- Lifestyle expenses (dining out, hobbies, entertainment)
- Health and wellness (gym memberships, healthcare costs)

Questions to Ask

- Where did you overspend compared to your budget (if you had one)?
- Which expenses brought high value and satisfaction?
- Which expenses were regrettable or underutilized?
- How do your expenses align with your values and goals?

Action Items

- Identify 2–3 expense categories to trim in the coming year.
- Plan for upcoming major expenses—licensing renewals, equipment upgrades.
- Build a "future fund" for big-ticket items instead of using debt.

Step 3: Savings and Investment Check

Gather Your Data

Collect year-end statements from:

- Savings accounts
- Checking accounts
- Brokerage accounts
- Retirement accounts (401(k), 403(b), IRA, SEP IRA, Solo 401(k))
- Health savings accounts (HSA)

Questions to Ask

- What's your total savings rate as a percentage of gross income?
- How much did you contribute to retirement accounts? Did you max out contributions?
- Are your investments appropriately diversified?
- Are your asset allocations aligned with your time horizon and risk

tolerance?
- Have you rebalanced your portfolio in the last year?

Action Items

- Increase your savings rate by 1–2% if possible.
- Review your asset allocation—adjust if you're too heavily weighted in one area.
- If you're behind on retirement savings, set up automatic contribution increases.

Step 4: Debt and Liability Review

Gather Your Data

Make a list of all current debts:

- Mortgage
- Car loans
- Credit card balances
- Student loans
- Personal loans
- Business loans (if applicable)

Include the balance, interest rate, and monthly payment for each.

Questions to Ask

- Has your total debt load increased or decreased?
- Are you paying down high-interest debt aggressively?
- Are you refinancing opportunities to lower interest rates?
- Are you managing your debt strategically (e.g., debt snowball or avalanche method)?

Action Items

- Prioritize paying off the highest-interest debts first.
- Consider consolidating or refinancing loans if it reduces your interest rate.
- Set a target debt reduction number for the next year.

Step 5: Insurance and Risk Management Review

Gather Your Data

Review policies for:

- Health insurance
- Disability insurance
- Life insurance
- Professional liability insurance
- Business insurance
- Auto and home insurance

Questions to Ask

- Are your coverage amounts still appropriate?
- Are there any gaps in coverage (e.g., no umbrella liability insurance)?
- Are you paying competitive premiums?
- Do you have updated beneficiaries on life insurance policies?

Action Items

- Increase coverage if your family or business situation has changed.
- Shop for competitive quotes to potentially lower premiums.
- Add riders or endorsements if necessary (e.g., business interruption insurance).

Step 6: Goal Alignment and Future Planning

Gather Your Data

Review:

- Written financial goals (if you have them).
- Business and career goals.
- Life goals—buying a home, starting a family, launching a side project.

Questions to Ask

- Did you meet the financial goals you set last year?
- Are your goals still relevant, or have they changed?
- Are you on track for longer-term goals like retirement or financial independence?
- What personal or professional milestones are on the horizon?

Action Items

- Set 3–5 financial goals for the next year.
- Break goals into quarterly action steps.
- Build in regular check-ins (quarterly or semi-annual) to monitor progress.

Sample Annual Review Template

You can use the following simple template as a framework:

Income Summary

- Salary:
- Bonus:
- Freelance Income:

- Investment Income:
- Total Income:

Expense Summary

- Essentials:
- Discretionary:
- Business:
- Total Expenses:

Savings and Investments

- Emergency Fund Balance:
- Retirement Accounts:
- Brokerage Accounts:
- Total Savings Rate:

Debt Summary

- Mortgage Balance:
- Student Loans:
- Credit Cards:
- Total Debt:

Insurance Review

- Health:
- Disability:
- Life:
- Professional Liability:
- Business:

Goals for Next Year

1.
2.
3.

Notes and Reflections

- Wins:
- Lessons Learned:
- Changes to Make:

Turning Financial Reviews Into a Habit

The first time you do a financial review, it might feel overwhelming. But, like any new skill—CAD modeling, client presentations, construction detailing—it gets easier and faster with practice.

Schedule It: Block off a full day once a year—perhaps right after tax season when your financial documents are already organized.

Make It a Ritual: Pair it with something enjoyable. Go to your favorite coffee shop, take a personal retreat day, or make it an annual tradition with your spouse or partner.

Document Progress: Keep copies of each year's review so you can track progress over time.

Revisit Quarterly: While the annual review is deep and comprehensive, short quarterly check-ins can keep you on track.

Mindset: Building a Resilient Financial Structure

Approach your finances with the same mindset you bring to designing a building:

- **Start with a strong foundation** (emergency fund, insurance, basic investing).
- **Design for function and beauty** (financial systems that are simple,

effective, and sustainable).

- **Account for change** (life will throw curveballs—design for flexibility).
- **Maintain and adapt** (review and refine annually).

A building left unattended deteriorates. So does a financial plan. Regular, thoughtful attention ensures both stay strong and enduring.

Chapter 41: Final Word, Design Your Financial Life With Intention

Financial success isn't accidental. It's architected.

As architects, we are taught from day one to think intentionally about space. About flow. About the relationship between function and form. About the impact of small details on the human experience. Good design doesn't happen by chance—it's the result of deliberate planning, testing, iteration, and execution. The same is true of your financial life.

You can't leave your financial future to luck or inertia. You must design it. Carefully. Intentionally. Thoughtfully. You must approach your financial life with the same rigor, creativity, and discipline you bring to your design projects.

This final chapter is a call to action—to treat your financial life like the most important project you will ever design.

The Parallels Between Architecture and Financial Planning

An architect doesn't start designing by throwing random lines on paper. You begin with research, site analysis, client interviews, feasibility studies, and zoning reviews. You seek constraints and possibilities. You work within budgets and codes. You think both creatively and pragmatically.

Financial planning is no different. To design a successful financial life, you must:

- Research and understand your starting point.
- Clarify your personal values and goals (your "program").
- Set constraints (budgets, risk tolerance, time horizons).
- Develop schematics (financial plans and projections).
- Refine the design through iteration (regular reviews and adjustments).
- Execute with discipline and creativity.

Design and finance are not opposites. They are two sides of the same thoughtful process.

Step One: Define Success For Yourself

Success, in architecture and in life, is deeply personal.

For one architect, success might mean running a boutique design firm with a small, loyal clientele and ample time for travel and family. For another, it might mean designing landmark skyscrapers and building an international reputation. Financially, some may seek early retirement and financial independence by 50; others may aim to work well into their 70s because they love the craft.

What matters is that you define success on your terms.

Questions to Ask Yourself:

- What does financial freedom look like to me?
- How do I want to spend my time when I have choices?
- What balance do I want between work, family, creativity, and rest?
- What legacy do I want to leave behind?

Clarity here gives your financial blueprint a clear program to work from.

Step Two: Design From the End Goal Backwards

In architecture, we often work backwards. We imagine the completed building—the way it will feel, the way people will move through it, the way light will hit it at different times of the day—and we design toward that vision.

You can use the same approach with your finances. Start with the end in mind. Visualize your ideal financial life 10, 20, 30 years from now. Then work backward.

If you want to retire at 60 with a $2 million nest egg, you can calculate how much you need to save each year starting now. If you want to pay off your mortgage in 15 years instead of 30, you can structure your payments accordingly. If you want to start your own firm, you can reverse-engineer the capital you'll need to launch.

Work backwards from the life you want—not forwards from where you are.

Step Three: Build Systems, Not Just Goals

Goals are important, but systems are what get you there.

In architecture, we don't just set a goal to "build a building." We create systems—design systems, project management systems, QA/QC systems—that make the goal inevitable.

Similarly, don't just set a goal to "save more" or "spend less." Build systems:

- Automate retirement contributions.
- Set up monthly transfers to investment accounts.
- Use budgeting software or spreadsheets.
- Schedule quarterly financial check-ins.
- Create templates for project invoicing and cash flow management.

Systems reduce reliance on willpower. They create momentum. Over time, they compound, just like interest.

Step Four: Design for Resilience, Not Perfection

No building is immune to the forces of time, weather, or human error. We design for resilience—with redundancy, with strong foundations, with materials that can withstand stress.

Your financial plan needs resilience too.

- Have an emergency fund for economic downturns.
- Diversify your investments across asset classes.
- Maintain multiple income streams if possible.
- Insure against major risks—disability, liability, property loss.

Perfection is unattainable. Resilience is essential.

Step Five: Iterate and Evolve

The best architects don't cling rigidly to their first draft. They test. They get feedback. They revise. They adapt as conditions change.

Your financial plan should evolve too.

- Reassess your goals every year.
- Adjust your portfolio as you age.
- Rebalance your budget as your income grows.
- Update your estate plans after major life changes.

Financial planning isn't a "set it and forget it" exercise. It's a living document. An evolving blueprint. Just like a masterful design.

Step Six: Honor Both Function and Form

In architecture, we know that a building must be both functional and beautiful. It must serve the needs of its occupants while also inspiring them.

Your financial life should be the same.

It must be functional:

- Provide security and freedom.
- Fund your goals.
- Protect your family.

But it should also be beautiful:

- Allow for generosity and giving.
- Enable experiences that bring joy.
- Reflect your values and priorities.

A well-designed financial life is not just about spreadsheets and calculators. It's about living with intention and meaning.

Financial Success Is Intentional

Luck plays a role in everyone's life. So does randomness. But sustained financial success—the kind that spans careers and generations—is not an accident. It's architected.

It's the result of:

- Clear vision.
- Deliberate design.
- Thoughtful systems.
- Consistent iteration.
- Balanced priorities.

- Resilient structures.

The most successful architects are not just good designers. They are master planners. They balance creativity with discipline. They balance ambition with humility. They see the big picture but sweat the details.

You have those skills. You use them every day in your professional life. Now it's time to apply them to your personal finances.

Final Encouragement: You Are Capable

This book has given you the tools—the knowledge, the frameworks, the blueprints. But tools alone don't build a building. Architects do.

Similarly, information alone doesn't create financial success. Action does.

You don't have to be perfect. You just have to be intentional.

Remember:

- Every automatic transfer is a brick in your financial foundation.
- Every budget review is a window into your financial future.
- Every insurance policy is a beam supporting your financial structure.
- Every investment is a load-bearing column for your future freedom.

Build patiently. Build deliberately. Build beautifully.

You are more capable than you think—and you are building a future you can be proud of.

Your Next Steps

Before you close this book, take a few moments:

- Write down your top 3 financial goals for the next year.
- Identify one system you can implement this month.
- Schedule your next annual financial review.

- Share your intentions with someone you trust.

Financial planning isn't about being perfect. It's about laying the groundwork and refining it over time.

The smartest architects don't just design beautiful buildings—they design sustainable lives.

And just like the best buildings, the best lives are not accidental. They are architected.

With care. With creativity. With intention.Financial success isn't accidental. It's architected.

As architects, we are taught from day one to think intentionally about space. About flow. About the relationship between function and form. About the impact of small details on the human experience. Good design doesn't happen by chance—it's the result of deliberate planning, testing, iteration, and execution. The same is true of your financial life.

You can't leave your financial future to luck or inertia. You must design it. Carefully. Intentionally. Thoughtfully. You must approach your financial life with the same rigor, creativity, and discipline you bring to your design projects.

This final chapter is a call to action—to treat your financial life like the most important project you will ever design.

The Parallels Between Architecture and Financial Planning

An architect doesn't start designing by throwing random lines on paper. You begin with research, site analysis, client interviews, feasibility studies, and zoning reviews. You seek constraints and possibilities. You work within budgets and codes. You think both creatively and pragmatically.

Financial planning is no different. To design a successful financial life, you must:

- Research and understand your starting point.
- Clarify your personal values and goals (your "program").

- Set constraints (budgets, risk tolerance, time horizons).
- Develop schematics (financial plans and projections).
- Refine the design through iteration (regular reviews and adjustments).
- Execute with discipline and creativity.

Design and finance are not opposites. They are two sides of the same thoughtful process.

Step One: Define Success For Yourself

Success, in architecture and in life, is deeply personal.

For one architect, success might mean running a boutique design firm with a small, loyal clientele and ample time for travel and family. For another, it might mean designing landmark skyscrapers and building an international reputation. Financially, some may seek early retirement and financial independence by 50; others may aim to work well into their 70s because they love the craft.

What matters is that you define success on your terms.

Questions to Ask Yourself:

- What does financial freedom look like to me?
- How do I want to spend my time when I have choices?
- What balance do I want between work, family, creativity, and rest?
- What legacy do I want to leave behind?

Clarity here gives your financial blueprint a clear program to work from.

Step Two: Design From the End Goal Backwards

In architecture, we often work backwards. We imagine the completed building—the way it will feel, the way people will move through it, the way light will hit it at different times of the day—and we design toward that vision.

You can use the same approach with your finances. Start with the end in mind. Visualize your ideal financial life 10, 20, 30 years from now. Then work backward.

If you want to retire at 60 with a $2 million nest egg, you can calculate how much you need to save each year starting now. If you want to pay off your mortgage in 15 years instead of 30, you can structure your payments accordingly. If you want to start your own firm, you can reverse-engineer the capital you'll need to launch.

Work backwards from the life you want—not forwards from where you are.

Step Three: Build Systems, Not Just Goals

Goals are important, but systems are what get you there.

In architecture, we don't just set a goal to "build a building." We create systems—design systems, project management systems, QA/QC systems—that make the goal inevitable.

Similarly, don't just set a goal to "save more" or "spend less." Build systems:

- Automate retirement contributions.
- Set up monthly transfers to investment accounts.
- Use budgeting software or spreadsheets.
- Schedule quarterly financial check-ins.
- Create templates for project invoicing and cash flow management.

Systems reduce reliance on willpower. They create momentum. Over time, they compound, just like interest.

Step Four: Design for Resilience, Not Perfection

No building is immune to the forces of time, weather, or human error. We design for resilience—with redundancy, with strong foundations, with materials that can withstand stress.

Your financial plan needs resilience too.

- Have an emergency fund for economic downturns.
- Diversify your investments across asset classes.
- Maintain multiple income streams if possible.
- Insure against major risks—disability, liability, property loss.

Perfection is unattainable. Resilience is essential.

Step Five: Iterate and Evolve

The best architects don't cling rigidly to their first draft. They test. They get feedback. They revise. They adapt as conditions change.

Your financial plan should evolve too.

- Reassess your goals every year.
- Adjust your portfolio as you age.
- Rebalance your budget as your income grows.
- Update your estate plans after major life changes.

Financial planning isn't a "set it and forget it" exercise. It's a living document. An evolving blueprint. Just like a masterful design.

Step Six: Honor Both Function and Form

In architecture, we know that a building must be both functional and beautiful. It must serve the needs of its occupants while also inspiring them.

Your financial life should be the same.

It must be functional:

- Provide security and freedom.
- Fund your goals.
- Protect your family.

But it should also be beautiful:

- Allow for generosity and giving.
- Enable experiences that bring joy.
- Reflect your values and priorities.

A well-designed financial life is not just about spreadsheets and calculators. It's about living with intention and meaning.

Financial Success Is Intentional

Luck plays a role in everyone's life. So does randomness. But sustained financial success—the kind that spans careers and generations—is not an accident. It's architected.

It's the result of:

- Clear vision.
- Deliberate design.
- Thoughtful systems.
- Consistent iteration.
- Balanced priorities.
- Resilient structures.

The most successful architects are not just good designers. They are master planners. They balance creativity with discipline. They balance ambition with humility. They see the big picture but sweat the details.

You have those skills. You use them every day in your professional life. Now it's time to apply them to your personal finances.

Final Encouragement: You Are Capable

This book has given you the tools—the knowledge, the frameworks, the blueprints. But tools alone don't build a building. Architects do.

Similarly, information alone doesn't create financial success. Action does.

You don't have to be perfect. You just have to be intentional.

Remember:

- Every automatic transfer is a brick in your financial foundation.
- Every budget review is a window into your financial future.
- Every insurance policy is a beam supporting your financial structure.
- Every investment is a load-bearing column for your future freedom.

Build patiently. Build deliberately. Build beautifully.

You are more capable than you think—and you are building a future you can be proud of.

Your Next Steps

Before you close this book, take a few moments:

- Write down your top 3 financial goals for the next year.
- Identify one system you can implement this month.
- Schedule your next annual financial review.
- Share your intentions with someone you trust.

Financial planning isn't about being perfect. It's about laying the groundwork and refining it over time.

The smartest architects don't just design beautiful buildings—they design sustainable lives.

And just like the best buildings, the best lives are not accidental. They are architected.

With care. With creativity. With intention.

Questions to Ask a Financial Advisor, CPA, and Attorney (For Architects)

As an architect, you're trained to think critically, ask the right questions, and anticipate potential problems before they arise. When it comes to choosing financial professionals, the same mindset applies.

The stakes are high: You're not just looking for someone to manage your money—you're looking for a partner who understands the complexities of your career, compensation, and goals.

Here's a list of the questions you should ask financial advisors, CPAs, estate planning attorneys, and other key professionals to ensure you're building a financial support team that fits your life as an architect.

Questions to Ask a Financial Advisor (For Architects)

Are you a fiduciary 100% of the time?

Fiduciaries are legally required to put your best interests first—no commissions, no hidden agendas.

Do you have experience working with architects or creative professionals with similar income structures?

Architecture careers often include bonuses, fluctuating income from solo practice or side gigs, and firm ownership stakes. Make sure they understand the nuances.

How do you get paid?

Is it fee-only, fee-based, or commission-driven? You want clarity about whether they're earning money from selling you investment products or insurance.

Can you help with business-owner financial planning, firm succession, and equity partnerships?

If you own your practice, are a partner, or plan to be one, your financial picture is more complex than a salaried employee's.

Will you coordinate with my CPA, estate attorney, and other advisors?

A good advisor doesn't work in a vacuum. They collaborate to ensure your tax, legal, and investment strategies are aligned.

What is your investment philosophy?

Look for a clear, jargon-free answer. Evidence-based, diversified strategies should be the foundation—not hype or hot stock tips.

How do you help clients manage risk—especially professional liability and business continuity?

Architects face unique risks. Your advisor should understand insurance needs, contracts, and risk mitigation.

Can you advise on real estate investments or rental properties?

Many architects invest in real estate professionally and personally. An advisor who can model cash flows, cap rates, and tax consequences can add significant value.

Are you familiar with retirement planning for small business owners, including Solo 401(k)s, SEP IRAs, and Defined Benefit Plans?

If you own your firm or freelance, retirement planning options differ. Make sure they can explain them in plain English.

Do you provide financial modeling tools that show different future scenarios?

You want someone who can map out "if-then" outcomes—how different decisions impact your future wealth, much like architectural modeling.

Questions to Ask a CPA (Certified Public Accountant)

Do you work with architects, firm owners, or creative professionals?

Income types, tax deductions, and business structures for architects can be very different from other fields.

Do you offer proactive tax planning throughout the year—or just file returns?

You need someone who helps you lower your tax bill with ongoing strategies, not just someone who files once a year.

Are you experienced with multi-state taxation, self-employed income, or firm partnerships?

Architects working on projects across state lines or owning firms need someone familiar with complex filings.

Can you advise on maximizing deductions for business expenses—like software, travel, licensing fees, continuing education, and home offices?

Architects have specific deductible expenses. Make sure your CPA understands which ones apply to you.

Can you help optimize my retirement contributions for tax efficiency?

Good CPAs help you save today and plan for the future—whether it's 401(k)s, IRAs, HSAs, or other options.

Do you assist with tax strategies for real estate investments or rental properties?

If you invest in property, you need someone familiar with depreciation schedules, 1031 exchanges, and passive income rules.

Will you represent me if I'm audited?

Audit support matters. Know if your CPA has your back if the IRS ever calls.

Questions to Ask an Estate Planning Attorney

Do you specialize in working with architects or professionals with business ownership?

You want someone who understands firm ownership, professional licenses, and asset protection strategies.

What key documents should I have?

Will, living trust, durable power of attorney, and healthcare directive are foundational.

Can you help protect my assets from lawsuits or business risks?

Architects, especially those running their own firms, face exposure to legal risks. Asset protection strategies matter.

How do you structure estate plans for business owners or real estate investors?

Firm ownership and property investments require careful planning to avoid costly estate issues.

Should I consider a revocable living trust?

For many architects, a trust simplifies passing on assets and avoiding probate.

Can you help with planning for minor children, blended families, or special needs dependents?

If your family structure is complex, your estate plan should reflect that.

How often should I update my estate plan?

Your estate plan should grow as your wealth, family, and firm do.

Are you willing to coordinate with my financial planner and CPA?

Collaboration between your financial, tax, and legal advisors leads to the best results.

Questions to Ask a Business Attorney (For Architects Who Own Firms)

Do you work with architects, designers, or professional services firms?

Architecture firms have unique contracts, risk profiles, and IP considerations.

Can you help me form an LLC, S-Corp, or partnership—and explain the pros and cons for my situation?

The right entity structure can protect you and save on taxes.

Will you review or draft contracts—client agreements, employment contracts, NDAs, or licensing agreements?

Good contracts are crucial to protecting your firm and personal assets.

Can you advise on intellectual property protection—logos, designs, plans?

Your creative work has value. Protect it.

Can you help set up succession planning or exit strategies?

If you want to retire, sell, or transition the firm, planning starts years in advance.

How do you support liability protection for firm owners?

Architects face professional liability. You need someone who understands how to shield you and your firm.

Do you charge hourly, per project, or by retainer?

Clear pricing avoids surprises.

Bonus: Questions to Ask Other Professionals

Insurance Agent (Life, Disability, Umbrella, Liability)

- Are you independent or tied to specific companies?
- Can you explain disability insurance tailored to architects' income variability?
- Do I need an umbrella policy to cover my home, investments, or business exposure?
- Can you review my current coverage for gaps or overlaps?
- Should I have term or permanent life insurance?

Real Estate Advisor or Investment Property Specialist

- Can you evaluate rental properties based on cash flow and ROI analysis?
- What markets align with my long-term investment goals?
- Can you advise on tax benefits like depreciation and 1031 exchanges?

Architectural Career Coach or Business Consultant

- Can you help me structure a long-term career plan or firm succession strategy?
- How do you assist architects facing burnout or planning a transition to semi-retirement?
- Can you model the financial impact of advanced degrees, certifications, or a career pivot?

Final Thought

Choosing the right financial professionals is one of the highest-leverage decisions you can make.

Ask good questions.

Expect clear, respectful answers.

You wouldn't hire a contractor without vetting them.

Treat your financial life with the same care—and build a team worthy of your blueprint.

Disclaimer

Financial Literacy for Architects is written with the intent to educate, empower, and encourage architects at all stages of their careers to take control of their financial lives. The insights in this book are based on the author's personal experience, professional training, and over two decades of work in financial services, personal finance education, and advising professionals with creative and technical backgrounds.

That said, it's important to be clear about what this book is—and what it is not.

Educational Purpose Only

All content in this book is presented for general educational and informational purposes. It is designed to provide architects—whether just entering the workforce, moving toward firm ownership, navigating mid-career transitions, or planning retirement—with essential financial concepts, strategic tools, and awareness of the opportunities and challenges that come with a creative, high-responsibility career.

While this book shares frameworks, strategies, case studies, and real-world examples, it is not personalized financial advice. It should not be used as a substitute for professional consultation. Every architect's financial situation is unique. Your goals, compensation structure (salary, bonus, firm profits), business interests, family obligations, risk tolerance, and financial position must all be considered carefully.

Before making major financial, legal, or business decisions, you should work with licensed professionals who understand your specific needs and goals.

No Legal Advice

Although many architects deal with contracts, firm ownership structures, partnership agreements, real estate investments, and intellectual property matters, this book does not provide legal advice. It is not a replacement for working with a qualified attorney.

If you are:

- Negotiating a client or employment contract
- Structuring or dissolving a firm partnership
- Managing intellectual property rights for your designs
- Protecting yourself from liability
- Creating wills, trusts, or other estate planning documents

...you should seek the advice of an attorney who specializes in contract law, business law, intellectual property, or estate planning. Legal requirements and protections vary by state, country, and the specifics of your situation. You are responsible for understanding and complying with all applicable laws and regulations.

No Financial or Investment Advice

This book covers important topics like budgeting, firm cash flow, retirement planning, investing, taxes, and long-term wealth-building—from an educational standpoint, not an advisory one.

This book is not written by a Certified Financial Planner™, Registered Investment Advisor, or broker-dealer. The examples, sample budgets, and financial strategies discussed are general in nature and may not apply directly to your circumstances.

Before implementing any financial strategy, making investments, or changing your financial plans, consult a licensed financial professional—ideally one who understands the unique financial challenges and opportunities faced by architects.

Your firm's retirement plan, profit-sharing setup, personal investments, or real estate holdings are too important to leave to guesswork or generic advice.

No Accounting or Tax Advice

Taxes are a critical part of building and preserving wealth, especially for architects with firm ownership stakes, real estate investments, or freelance consulting income. However, this book is not written by a CPA, Enrolled Agent, or licensed tax preparer. Any discussion of tax deductions, brackets, or IRS rules is intended for general educational purposes only.

If you:

- Run your own firm or work as an independent contractor
- Invest in commercial or residential real estate
- Receive income across state lines or internationally
- Hold ownership in multiple entities or partnerships
- Need help with business deductions, depreciation, or advanced tax strategies

...you should hire a qualified tax professional. Only a licensed tax advisor can review your specific situation, help you comply with current tax laws, and develop personalized strategies to optimize your outcomes.

No Guarantees or Promises

Reading this book does not guarantee financial success, high investment returns, early retirement, or any specific outcome. Financial literacy is not a one-time achievement—it is a continuous practice that requires discipline, learning, and strategic action over time.

The examples and case studies provided are intended for illustration purposes only. They are not promises or predictions. Your financial outcomes will depend on many variables—your decisions, market conditions, economic cycles, health, life events, and sometimes luck.

Limitation of Liability

By reading this book, you agree that the author, Pat Brown, MBA, and all affiliated websites and brands—such as FinancialLiteracyForArchitects.com and FinancialLiteracyForNIL.com—are not responsible for your financial outcomes, legal disputes, or tax consequences.

Neither the author nor any associated entity shall be held liable for any financial losses, legal actions, tax penalties, or other negative results connected to your use of the information in this book. You are fully responsible for your financial decisions and actions.

Encouragement to Build Your Professional Team

It is the sincere belief of the author that every architect—whether you're designing skyscrapers, small homes, public spaces, or commercial developments—deserves a strong team of financial professionals:

- A financial advisor
- A tax advisor
- An estate planning attorney
- An insurance specialist

This book is designed to complement your professional team—not replace it.

If you haven't built your team yet, now is the time. Architects understand better than most the power of planning, structural integrity, systems thinking, and intentional design. Your financial life deserves the same rigor and attention you bring to your professional work.

You've spent years learning how to solve complex design problems, lead projects, and shape the built environment. Now it's time to ensure you architect a financial life that's as resilient, functional, and beautiful as the spaces you create.

Annual Financial Planning Calendar for Architects

Managing your finances well is like managing a long-term architecture project: it requires deadlines, milestones, and routine inspections. Use this month-by-month guide as a template to structure your financial year with intention.

JANUARY

January 1

- New contribution limits for 401(k), 403(b), 457, and IRA/Roth IRA accounts go into effect.
- Health Savings Account (HSA) and Flexible Spending Account (FSA) limits reset.
- Begin your new year's budget and cash flow review.
- Update paycheck withholding (Form W-4) if you've experienced life changes (marriage, divorce, children, etc.).

January 15

- Fourth Quarter Estimated Taxes Due (for income earned from October 1 to December 31 of the prior year). Use IRS Form 1040-ES.

Late January

- W-2s, 1099-NEC, 1099-MISC, 1099-INT, 1099-DIV, and 1099-B forms begin arriving from employers, banks, brokerages, and freelance clients.

FEBRUARY

February 1

- Deadline for employers and payers to issue W-2s and 1099s to employees and independent contractors.

Mid to Late February

- K-1 forms for partnerships or S-Corporations start arriving. Some may extend into March or April.
- Begin gathering documents for tax preparation—income forms, deductible expenses, investment statements, real estate documents, etc.

MARCH

March 15

- Tax deadline for Partnerships and S-Corporations (Form 1065 or 1120-S).
- Can file an extension using IRS Form 7004.

March 31

- Deadline to receive Form 1095-A, 1095-B, or 1095-C (health insurance coverage documentation) electronically.

APRIL

April 1

- Required Minimum Distributions (RMDs) must begin if you turned 73 last year and delayed your first withdrawal.

April 15 (or next business day if it falls on a weekend/holiday)

- Personal Tax Filing Deadline (IRS Form 1040).
- First Quarter Estimated Taxes Due.
- Deadline to make prior-year contributions to:
- Traditional IRA / Roth IRA
- SEP IRA (if not on extension)
- HSA
- Coverdell Education Savings Account (ESA)
- Last day to file for a 6-month extension (Form 4868).
- FAFSA filing deadline for many states (if applying for financial aid for children).

MAY

Early May

- Review property tax assessments if applicable. Protest deadlines typically fall mid-May depending on your jurisdiction.

May 29 (5/29 Day)

- National reminder to open or review 529 College Savings Plans for children or grandchildren.

JUNE

June 15

- Second Quarter Estimated Taxes Due.
- U.S. citizens living abroad must file taxes unless they request an extension to October 15.

Mid-June

- Mid-year performance review for retirement accounts. Adjust contributions if needed.
- Reassess charitable giving plans and donor-advised fund contributions for the year.

JULY

July 1–15

- Mid-year financial check-in:
- Review spending habits.
- Assess progress toward savings goals.
- Evaluate debt paydown progress.
- Rebalance your portfolio if any asset class has deviated by more than 5–10% from your target allocation.
- Schedule a check-in meeting with your financial advisor or CPA.

AUGUST

August 1–31

- Begin preparing for Open Enrollment (typically starts in October or November).
- Review HSA/FSA balances and ensure funds will be used efficiently.
- Review and update insurance coverage: life, disability, malpractice, and umbrella liability policies.
- Plan for year-end charitable giving strategies: Donor-Advised Funds, appreciated stock donations, Qualified Charitable Distributions (if 70½+).

SEPTEMBER

September 15

- Third Quarter Estimated Taxes Due.
- Final deadline for Calendar-Year Partnership and S-Corp tax returns

if on extension.

Late September

- Check Backdoor Roth IRA contributions and conversions.
- Consider tax-loss harvesting strategies before Q4 ends.

OCTOBER

October 1

- Deadline to establish a SIMPLE IRA for the current tax year (ideal for small firm owners).
- Medicare Open Enrollment preview window begins—important for retired architects or for parents/grandparents under your care.

October 15

- Extended Individual Tax Return Due Date (Form 1040 with extension).
- Final deadline to fund SEP IRA contributions for the prior year (if on tax extension).
- Deadline to recharacterize prior-year Roth IRA contributions if necessary.

Late October

- Review your Open Enrollment materials for employer-sponsored insurance.
- Evaluate health insurance options and adjust life and disability insurance as needed.

NOVEMBER

November 1–30

- Health Insurance Open Enrollment opens for ACA Marketplace.
- Employer benefits enrollment typically opens:
- Review health plan options (consider HSA-eligible plans).
- Review life and disability insurance.
- Update 401(k) contribution elections.
- Adjust FSA/HSA elections.
- Consider legal services, vision/dental coverage, or supplemental benefits.

Black Friday Weekend

- If planning large purchases (equipment, technology upgrades, etc.), review cash flow and timing around year-end budgeting.

DECEMBER

December 1–15

- Last call to maximize retirement contributions:
- 401(k), 403(b), 457 contributions
- HSA contributions (via payroll deduction)
- Backdoor Roth IRA conversions

December 31

- Final day for:
- Charitable contributions to count toward current year taxes (be mindful of DAF deadlines).
- Tax-loss harvesting strategies.
- Taking Required Minimum Distributions (RMDs) if age 73 or older.
- Annual gifting up to $18,000 per recipient without gift tax filing requirements.
- Spending down FSA funds (check for grace period or rollover policies).
- Completing Roth IRA conversions.

- Issuing bonuses or profit-sharing contributions if operating an S-Corporation.

Bonus: Rolling & Event-Based Reminders

Every Paycheck

- Verify 401(k)/403(b) deductions and elections.
- Check HSA contributions.
- Confirm proper withholding on health, dental, and vision premiums.

After Major Life Events

- Marriage or divorce
- Birth or adoption of a child
- Starting a new job or freelance contract
- Disability or health changes
- Change of primary residence
- Inheritance or major financial windfall

Quarterly

- Review and adjust your budget and spending habits.
- Make estimated tax payments if necessary.
- Review investment performance and rebalance as needed.
- Consult with your advisor on tax planning opportunities such as loss harvesting or Roth conversions.

Final Tip: Automate Where Possible

Financial discipline thrives on automation:

- Set up calendar reminders.

- Automate savings and investment contributions.
- Establish recurring debt payments.
- Schedule annual reviews.

The fewer tasks you leave to memory or chance, the more consistent and effective your financial plan will be—just like a well-designed project running on time and under budget.

Financial Literacy Resources for Architects

Architects are skilled at designing structures that endure—but too often, the blueprint for financial success is missing from professional training. Whether you're just beginning your architectural career or are an experienced firm owner thinking about retirement, the right financial education can help you design a life that is not only sustainable but also prosperous.

Here is a curated list of resources tailored to help architects at every stage of their journey.

Financial Literacy for Architects

A dedicated platform offering practical guides, tools, and educational resources tailored to the financial lives of architects—from entry-level designers to seasoned firm principals.

The Architect's Guide to Financial Mastery

An insightful article providing strategies for architects to achieve financial independence, covering essential topics like budgeting, investing, debt management, and retirement planning.

ARQ Wealth Advisors – Financial Planning Tips for Architects

Expert advice on maximizing 401(k) and HSA contributions, optimizing firm profitability, protecting income with insurance, and building a resilient financial foundation.

Personal Finance for Architects – Architecture.com

A comprehensive guide discussing key financial principles, including asset management, tax strategies for project-based income, and sustainable wealth-building techniques.

Financial Acumen for Architects – Architecture Education Aus-

tralia

A course aimed at enhancing architects' financial decision-making skills, focusing on budgeting, cash flow management, financial reporting for firm owners, and investment analysis.

Financial Literacy for Architecture Graduates – OTM Online

Provides budgeting tools and resources to help new architecture graduates manage living expenses, student loans, and financial goal setting as they transition into their careers.

The Architect's Guide to Financial Planning – Lakewood Wealth

Discusses how architects can build wealth with precision, emphasizing goal setting, long-term planning, data analysis, and diversified investment strategies.

Financial Planning Challenges for Architects – Bollin Wealth Management

Highlights common financial hurdles architects face—such as irregular income, delayed earnings from project payments, and career volatility—offering solutions to manage cash flow and taxes effectively.

Financial Literacy for Architects – MRS Fall Meeting & Exhibit

A presentation introducing fundamental financial concepts tailored to architecture and design students, helping future architects build a strong financial foundation early.

Financial Literacy Modules for Architects – University of Iowa

Educational modules covering essential financial concepts like interest, present value, and budgeting, integrating business fundamentals with design thinking.

WorldQuant University – MSc in Financial Engineering

Offers a free, accredited online master's program focused on quantitative finance—ideal for architects interested in enhancing their financial acumen for firm ownership or real estate development ventures.

Corporate Finance Institute (CFI)

Provides online courses and certifications in financial modeling, valuation, and corporate finance, suitable for architects looking to develop stronger business and financial analysis skills.

Investopedia – Financial Literacy Resources

A comprehensive platform offering tutorials, articles, and tools to build financial knowledge across investing, budgeting, tax planning, and wealth management topics.

Wall Street Survivor

An educational website using gamification to teach investing and personal finance concepts—allowing architects to practice building virtual portfolios without risk.

Next Gen Personal Finance (NGPF)

Offers free courses and resources in personal finance, an excellent supplement for architects wanting to strengthen their financial literacy in areas like saving, investing, and debt management.

Federal Reserve Education

Provides accessible educational materials on economics, markets, and personal finance—helping architects understand broader financial systems and how they affect long-term planning.

Financial Literacy and the Architect – YouTube Webinar

A webinar introducing foundational financial concepts tailored for architects, covering budgeting, saving for retirement, and building passive income streams.

Refactoring – Personal Finance for Architects

An article discussing the importance of financial planning for architects, offering practical strategies on managing inconsistent income, setting aside tax reserves, and investing with discipline.

Engineering Financial Literacy – Stanford d.school

Though focused on engineers, this initiative highlights design-thinking approaches to financial literacy that architects can adapt to solve money management challenges creatively.

Financial Planning for Architects – Scripted.com

A guide outlining the necessary steps for architects to create effective, sustainable financial plans, with an emphasis on budgeting, risk management, and long-term wealth-building.

These resources are designed to empower architects with the knowledge and tools necessary to make informed financial decisions throughout their careers—whether they are designing iconic buildings, running successful firms, or preparing for a well-earned retirement.

About the Author

Patrick Brown, MBA, is a former Division I football player turned wealth advisor, educator, and nationally respected voice in financial literacy. With more than two decades of experience in financial planning, insurance, and investment strategy, Patrick has made it his mission to help individuals and families build wealth with clarity, confidence, and a long-term vision.

After earning his MBA and launching a successful career in wealth management, Patrick created a series of financial literacy platforms aimed at educating overlooked and underserved communities. These include:

- *Financial Literacy For NIL*
- *Financial Literacy For Student Athletes*
- *Financial Literacy For The Culture*
- *Financial Literacy For College Coaches*
- *Financial Literacy For Parents of Student Athletes*

Now, through *Financial Literacy For Architects*, Patrick brings his mission to one of the most design-driven, systems-oriented professions in the world. Architects are renowned for solving complex spatial problems, creating enduring structures, and designing human experiences—but many have never been taught how to apply that same rigor and precision to their personal finances. Patrick's goal is to change that.

His passion for financial education is rooted in personal experience. Raised in a home where money was rarely discussed, he saw firsthand how financial insecurity and silence around money matters could derail promising futures. He's committed to bridging the gap between earning income and building sustainable, generational wealth.

Over the years, Patrick has become a trusted advisor to a diverse range of clients—including architects, engineers, physicians, student-athletes, entrepreneurs, retirees, and young professionals. His approach is practical, culturally aware, and grounded in real-life scenarios—not jargon or hype. Whether you're a recent architecture school graduate stepping into your first firm, a mid-career principal balancing practice leadership with personal goals, or a seasoned architect preparing for a thoughtful retirement, Patrick's advice is designed to meet you where you are and help you move forward—strategically.

Outside of his financial work, Patrick is deeply involved in community leadership. He serves as a Trustee on the Board of Lawrence Memorial Hospital (LMH) and participates in hospital board committees focused on governance, strategic planning, and patient outcomes. He also serves on several nonprofit and civic boards across the region, advocating for financial literacy, family support, and healthcare access.

Above all, Patrick is a proud husband and father. When he's not helping others navigate their financial lives, he enjoys speaking at architecture schools, community events, and professional organizations—translating financial education into stories that resonate and strategies that work.

Patrick believes financial literacy is about more than just dollars and cents—it's about creating options, building freedom, and designing a life you're proud to live. Just as architects transform ideas into enduring structures, Patrick empowers individuals to transform income into lasting wealth and security.

Final Word

Need Help? Start Here

This book exists because financial education is a powerful tool. When used well, it can open doors, protect your legacy, and give you the confidence to take control of your future.

But just like architecture, success isn't built through guesswork. You need structure. You need systems. You need the ability to ask the right questions, evaluate trade-offs, and know when to bring in specialists. It's not about mastering every single detail—it's about navigating decisions with clarity and confidence.

Use this book as a guide—not a rule book. Let it inspire action. Let it help you build momentum. But don't treat it as a substitute for professional advice. Be curious. Stay informed. Keep asking good questions before making any major financial decisions.

Trusted Resources

If you're looking for guidance or just want to talk through your next steps, reach out to professionals who understand your world—design thinking, systems, and the pressure of making real-world decisions that endure.

Pat Brown, MBA

Wealth advisor. Financial literacy advocate. Former D1 athlete.

Advisor to architects, engineers, student-athletes, and high-performing professionals nationwide.

Website: www.financialliteracyforarchitects.com

Email: info@financialliteracyforarchitects.com

Join Our Newsletter

Stay updated with insights, strategies, and reminders that help you stay financially sharp—delivered directly to your inbox.

Final Word: Use This. Don't Shelf It.

These tools aren't meant to collect dust or sit unread in the back of a drawer. Use them. Revisit them. Share them with someone who needs them. Apply what works, test what doesn't, and keep refining your process.

This is your playbook for life—professionally, personally, and financially.

Stay sharp. Stay curious. Keep architecting a better future.

Working with a Financial Advisor: Is It the Right Move for an Architect?

As an architect, you're trained to balance vision with precision, creativity with structure, art with engineering. You solve complex design problems daily, manage projects, lead teams, and make high-stakes decisions. Yet when it comes to your personal finances, you may wonder whether it makes sense to manage it all yourself—or bring in a professional to help oversee the big picture.

The reality? Working with a financial advisor can offer tremendous value, especially for architects juggling demanding careers, variable incomes, high earnings, or complex long-term goals. But just like any good design project, it's important to weigh the pros and cons before committing.

Pros of Working with a Financial Advisor

1. Cross-Disciplinary Expertise

A qualified financial advisor brings broad expertise—investing, tax strategy, insurance, risk management, estate planning, retirement modeling. For architects with fluctuating project-based income, self-employment dynamics, or ownership stakes in firms, this integrated view is crucial for long-term success.

2. Time-Saving and Stress-Reducing

Your days are filled with deadlines, client meetings, design reviews, and site visits. Researching backdoor Roth IRAs, evaluating health savings account strategies, or projecting retirement income may not make your priority list. Delegating this work to a trusted advisor saves time, reduces mental load, and frees up bandwidth for what matters most—your practice, your creativity, your life.

3. Rational, Objective Guidance

Even the most logical architects are human. Market drops, project cancellations, unexpected windfalls—life happens. An advisor can act as a buffer between emotion and action, helping you zoom out, avoid rash decisions, and stay focused on the long-term plan when things get turbulent.

4. Accountability and Follow-Through

Designers understand systems. But building and maintaining a financial system—insurance coverage, estate plans, retirement contributions—takes ongoing attention. An advisor ensures that the easy-to-ignore tasks, like updating beneficiaries or rebalancing investments, actually get done. They serve not just as planners but as accountability partners.

5. Customized Planning That Fits You

A solid financial advisor doesn't push a templated plan. They ask about your firm structure, licensing goals, real estate ambitions, family needs, and long-term creative and professional vision. Whether you're a firm principal contemplating succession or an associate trying to build wealth while repaying loans, good advice should fit your life and values.

Cons of Working with a Financial Advisor

1. The Cost

Advisors charge for their services—usually a percentage of assets (commonly 0.5%–1%), a flat fee, or an hourly rate. For architects early in their careers or just starting to invest, these fees might feel like an obstacle. It's essential to understand the fee structure and ensure the services offered justify the price.

2. Quality and Transparency Aren't Universal

Not all advisors are created equal. Some are fiduciaries legally required to act in your best interest; others are commission-based brokers or insurance salespeople. You need to ask the tough questions, demand transparency, and ensure you're working with someone whose incentives align with yours.

3. It's Not "Set It and Forget It"

Even with a great advisor, you can't completely outsource the responsibility. Big financial decisions—around risk, career changes, succession planning, major purchases—still require your involvement. An advisor steers the ship, but you're the captain.

4. Risk of Generic, Templated Advice

Some advisors rely on canned portfolios and cookie-cutter plans. If they don't understand the nuances of architectural practice—like project-based cash flow, delayed payments, retirement savings gaps, or firm ownership transitions—they might not be the right fit. Architects deserve precision and customization.

5. You Might Not Need One—Yet

If you're financially literate, enjoy managing your money, and have relatively simple needs—steady W-2 income, basic retirement savings, no dependents—you might be fine on your own for now. Automation tools, low-cost index funds, and solid financial habits can carry you a long way.

So... Should You Hire a Financial Advisor?

Ask yourself these questions:

- Do I have the time, tools, and discipline to manage my finances consistently?
- Am I confident in my investment, tax, and protection strategies?
- Do I feel overwhelmed or stuck trying to prioritize financial decisions?
- Am I making full use of my employer or firm benefits, retirement plans, and tax strategies?
- Would having a guide increase my peace of mind and help me avoid costly mistakes?

If you answered "no" to one or more of these, an advisor might be worth considering. The best ones don't just manage your portfolio—they educate you, strategize with you, and help align your financial plan with the life you're designing.

In the end, it's no different from architecture itself: the best structures are created with expertise, collaboration, careful planning—and a willingness to bring in specialists when the stakes are high.

Made in the USA
Monee, IL
04 November 2026

67386762R00236